WINGS OF LEGACY

Chronicles Of College,
Family, And The
Navy Through Letters
Home

BOOK 2

RICHARD CHERBA

Color vs Black and White

Some photos that appear in this book were submitted in color but were printed in black and white. This choice was made due to printing costs not only for the author but by future customers. So with help, an image gallery website is available to view these photos in color.

https://drive.google.com/drive/folders/1qx8IS707UbyR1D-9s5WlVxNqqmuqyY2P?usp=drive_link

DEDICATION

To my Mother. Irene Cherba who kept every letter and mail that I sent home from college and the Navy. organized, them by date and put them in folders by year so that they would not get lost. Stored in a banker's box.

My Mom, 1946

Copyright Page

Wings of Legacy- © Copyright

<<2024>> Richard Cherba

ISBN:

PREFACE

My book is actually in two volumes, 1 and 2. The publishers would not accept my manuscript due to the length. So I made the decision to split the document in half and thus it became 2 books. Nothing has been left out of the original manuscript. The book's length is over 900 pages.

The years cover 1956 thru1967.

Thanks,

Dick

INDEX

1963   11
18 Letters 1/6/63 - 12/25/63

1964   63
23 Letters 1/12/64 - 12/20/64

1965   119
27 Letters 1/25/65 - 12/30/65

1966   199
7 Letters 2/23/66 - 12/30/66

1967   215
6 Letters 1/6/67 - 8/4/67

Joined Navy, Cadet, Ensign Commission   231

Training Begins, Various Photos   237

Designated Naval Aviator, Wings of Gold   242

Started A-4 training, Touring photos   245

Sea Stories, TR-3 accident, post cards   275

Viet Nam Prisoners, Air Refueling   306

USS Midway by the numbers, True Sea stories   321

Advance to Lieutenant, Stories, Separation Orders   347

Cartoons, Air Medal, Discharge, Diary   427

Pam/Oick Marriage, New Family Member   435

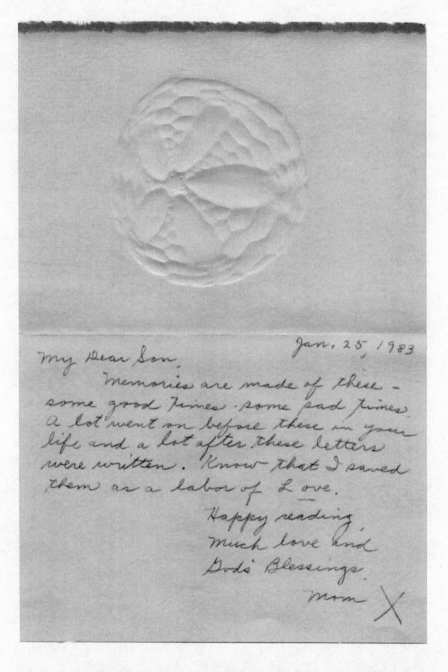

LETTERS 1956-1967

LETTERS

**From Richard Cherba
to My Parents John & Irene Cherba
From US NAVY**

1963

USS MIDWAY

U.S. NAVAL AIR STATION
Lemoore, California

1963

6 Jan.

Dear Mom & Dad,

Just a few lines to say hello. I am feeling fine and hope everyone is well at home. I just got back from S.F., I spent the week end there just partying. That town has a little more night life than Fresno or Lemoore.

Well I got my leave from 19 to 25 of Jan. I have one major question and that is if you could loan me the money for the plane fare. If not I'll just borrow it from Navy Federal. It will be about $200.00. I leave L.A. on the 19th at 2:45 pm and arrive on flight #828 from Chicago at 11:02 in Cleve. I already have made reservations for the return also on the following Fri. as I must stand the duty on Sat the 26 and leave for Fallon on Sunday. The return leaves Cleveland at 9:00 AM. Isme will be glad to get home for a few days.

That Xmas card from Lima was from Al Zoller. He is a salesman for the Shell Oil Co. and was transferred to that territory.

I see by the concert schedule that the B-W Band is having a concert at 8 pm on the Sunday that I will be home. If I don't get snowed in somewhere, why don't we plan to go. It will be good to hear the band again.

Well, I will close for now. Give Irene and family my hello.

love,
Richard

INTRODUCTION

The little British Crown Colony of Hong Kong, perched on the southernmost tip of China, is the greatest non-Communist Chinese city left in the world. It is the last outpost of traditional "Chinese-ness" with its virtues and faults, its teeming colorful strangeness.

Tourists describe Hong Kong as the biggest bargain counter in the world. This is a free port, so some goods cost even less than in their country of origin. Shops overflow with the finest textiles of Europe and Japan, ancient Buddha heads, lustrous Mikimoto pearls, German and Japanese tape recorders and cameras, Mongolian and Tibetan silver, Indian saris transparent as spider webs and weighted with bands of gold, silks alive and vibrant with color, hand-loomed in Thailand.

There are two parts to the British Colony. Hong Kong is 29 miles of rocky island pushing almost straight up from blue, gray, and violet seas. The other half of Hong Kong consists of more than 300 square miles of the China mainland (called the New Territories). Its tip, Kowloon, almost four and a half square miles of shops, new buildings, and busy bustle, is about a five minute, three-to-four-cent ferry ride from Hong Kong Island, across one of the world's most magnificent harbors.

28 JAN

Dear Mom & Dad,

Well here I am in Fallon already. The trip back to L.A. wasn't too bad except for leaving Cleveland a little late. It took about an hour to get to Chicago where I had to wait ½ hour to catch my connection.

From L.A. I took a Greyhound bus back which took about 6½ hours. I didn't want to chance the fog here in the valley.

I enjoyed my stay at home and just being there, although it was short. Thank you for all that you did for me. I enjoyed everything.

We left for Fallon by car (4 of us) at 9:30 AM Sunday. We stopped at Harrah's for a while and tried to see NAT Cole but he was all sold out. We had dinner in Carson City and arrived here at 9:30 p.m. We had a good time driving up here.

There still isn't any snow up here and the ski lodges are going broke. This certainly is a bad year for them.

Well I was up at 6 AM this morning and I'm tired after flying today, so I think I'll read a bit then go to bed. I'll write again next week.

Love,
Richard

17 FEB

Dear Mom & Dad,

I am fine and hope everyone at home is OK too. Is the cold weather still with you? We have had a lot of rain in the past two weeks and everything looks real green.

This past week I have been in the back seat of an F9 getting my instrument card renewed.

Haven't been doing too much recently. Sat. nite I went in to Fresno to a Barber Shop concert. It was real good and wasn't a contest but just for the fun of singing. They had several top quartets there from California.

All the military personnel are anxiously awaiting to see if Congress will vote our pay increase. We haven't had a pay increase (base pay other than longevity or promotion) since '54 (I think). The people of my pay grade will get an increase of $80.00

Some sailor was stabbed with a knife in Hanford by a 16 yr old kid. The sailor was minding his own when the groupthe was with was picked on. The sailor was killed. So as a result Hanford is off limits from 6 pm to 6 am. seven days a week. It's going to be another long hassle just like the housing problem except worse.

That picture of Brian sure is cute. Irene is good at writing clever little deals like that. I always get a kick out of her letters.

Here is part of the money I owe you. I will close for now.

Love,
Richard

U.S. NAVAL AIR STATION
Lemoore, California

24 FEB

Dear Mom & Dad,

It is a beautiful day out in the low 70's, very clear. Occasionally the fog returns but I think that it will start warming up soon. I am fine and hope you are the same. Today I have the duty. It has been fairly quiet although one of our enlisted men was in an auto accident, nothing serious.

Part of the squadron is going aboard the Hornet for CarQuals next week. There are 6 of us that are staying behind because we have qualled recently.

Played a dance job Sat. night in Hanford. Accordian, bass and drums. $20⁰⁰ It was a party for a squadron who is to deploy soon. VA-153. Our next deployment is back up to Fallon on April 22 for another two weeks.

I am thinking about renting the same cabin up at Bass Lake again this summer. However, it will have to be with 5 different guys as all of the regulars will be on cruise.

There is really not too much else going on around here so I will close for now.

Love,
Richard

11 March 1963

Dear Mom & Dad,

    I am fine and hope you are the same. The weather here has been real nice, up in the high 60's.

    The weekend of 2 MAR was a real thirsty one. We had a squadron party on Saturday night and we all really tied one on. This party was just for the officers. The party was a Bring your own bottle type and we polished those off. Lt Frank Peters, where we had the party, Barb. B. Q 60# of prime rib for chow with all the trimmings. It was real delicious. He also bought a small pony keg of beer which hardly was touched so he invited us all back to finish the beer and the rest of the rib on Sunday afternoon. I didn't come home until 11 pm.

    This last week-end on fun. a dentist buddy, who is now doing my dental work and I went on a drive to Sequoia, and hiked around a bit. Incidentally, in Feb. I took my annual physical, and was found to be in good health all the way around except for a little dental work by my bachelor buddy dentist who just got out of dental school a short while ago. I already have had two visits with 3 more to go. I haven't gone for at least 2 years. He does pretty good work.

This summer I am thinking about taking two weeks leave. I would like to go into Canada for some sightseeing or over to Yellowstone Nat'l Park. Our Squadron is going to be pretty busy though and I'm not sure whether or not I will get it.

Our next deployment is to Fallon again the last part of April and the first week in May.

I have two dance jobs coming up

IV will this combo from Hanford. Accordian, bass, and me. That is another $20.00 for each job.

By the way I did recieve the rolls. They were very good. The metal cans don't even survive the mails. It was bent out of shape. Haven't seen the Pearson's lately. Don't know how she is making out with the cook book.

I am returning the check. Please take it. I didn't borrow the money without knowing that I was going to pay it back.

Well I hope the fish are doing well. Gordon's basement probably looks like the Cleveland Aquarium. I'll close out for now until next time.

Love,
Richard

RICHARD CHERBA

24 MAR 63

Dear Mom + Dad,

Well here it is another beautiful Sunday with the sun out and kind of warm. I have the duty. This morning there wasn't a single cloud in the sky and the Sierra Mts and Coastal Ranges were clearly visible. Mt. Whitney was very beautiful with all the snow capped peaks. The ski lodges have been jammed to capacity the last few weekends.

I am fine just getting over one of my usual sniffles, and hope everything is A-OK at home.

Last weekend I flew up to Alameda with a plane for someone's use. I spent the weekend in S.F. and drove back in a Sprite (sports car) that Alvarez wrecked just before he went on cruise. It belongs to me & his shipmates wife. Sat. night I had dinner at Fisherman Giotto in Fisherman's Wharf. From there I proceeded direct to

Broadway and visited most of the taverns. I drove back on Sun. aft.

This last week we have been bowling in a tournament - everyday at 3:00pm. (1500) I bowled 3 games everyday and & my fingers are still sore, especially my thumb. It has a small callous on it.

Sat. night I had a dance job and we played at the ELKS in Hanford. Didn't get home until 2:30 and am a bit tired is we relieve the watch at 0800.

Mon. night the squadron is having an all Hands party at the Enlisted Men's Club. Free drinks, buffet, dancing and oh yes drinks (oh I already mentioned that!!). We get to sleep in on Tues. and don't have to be at work until noon.

Enclosed find second installment. Will close for now.

Love,
Richard

RICHARD CHERBA

21 April

Dear Mom & Dad

Please forgive me for not writing but it seems like I have just been a bit lazy and really not a whole lot to talk about. I am fine and hope everyone at home is OK too.

As you can see by the letter we are again at Fallon, Nev. for 2 weeks. Another gent and myself drove the XO's car up. Since I am number 14 in the squadron and we only brought 11 birds, a few of us had to drive. We left on the 24th and will return on 7 May. Then we go aboard ship for a few days for some carrier refreshers. On the way up we stopped at Lake Tahoe for a few hours and gave them some of our money. We left about 4 AM (Tahoe) to Fallon which is about a 2½ hour drive. We got a tad cold because the car didn't have any heater. It is a second car. But we both had sufficient clothing to keep us warm.

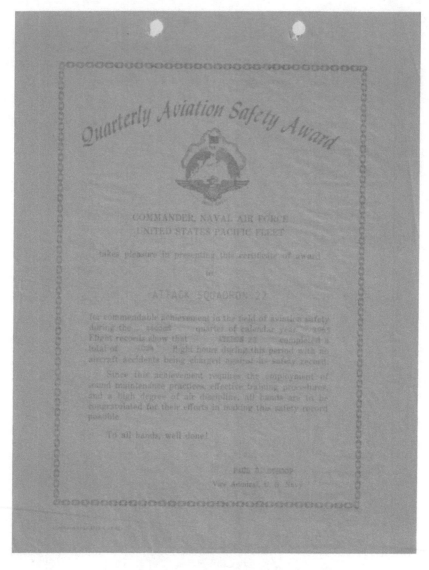

Quarterly Aviation Safety Award to VA 22
Second Quarter 1963, 1024 flight hours
First Quarter 1964, 1443 flight hours
Third Quarter 1964, 1363 flight hours
I have records of these 3 only

RICHARD CHERBA

A few week-ends ago a bachelor dentist friend of mine (who did all the recent dental work in my teeth) and I went to Las Vegas. He bought a new sport MGB and wanted to try it out. So we left about 5:45 p.m. Fri and it took us about 1½ hours to drive. We never went over 65 mph which is surprising for me but he wanted to break his car in. We got there and got a room at the Flamingo Hotel, got dressed and went out on the town got in about 8 am slept for 4 hrs. and started all over again. I came back a loser but had a good time. We saw the Juliet Prowse (Frank Sinatra's ex love) and Jackie Mason Show at the Flamingo Sat night.

Last weekend I went to Los Angeles to see Shirley Cherba and her friend. I borrowed a Volvo and took them around the Hollywood area. We took that same tour of the home which we all did last summer.

III

Then Sat night we went to Tijuana, Mex. (See vary picture) We took in the Jai Lai game. A fascinating sport and one also that money can be played on. I guess they left LA last night. They were there for two weeks, kind of disappointed with the city and the weather. It was chilly and they couldn't get any beach time. Their motel was right on the beach.

A couple of nights ago the gang went into Reno for some fun + frolic. This is the first time that I have actually been to Reno. It is called the biggest little city in the world and I can see why. I really don't care for it as much as Vegas though. There is a lot more to do and see in Vegas but I guess the tables are all the same. Like magnets that attract silver dollars.

At this very moment I am sitting on the approach end of the runway standing the Runway Duty Officer Watch (R.D.O) It is just a safety watch where you make sure that pilots land

RICHARD CHERBA

safely and with their gear down. I have been out here since 5:15 AM and due to be relieved at 0830.

Tonight I am proceeding via airlift to NAS MIRAMAR to pick up one of our birds there. I will return to Fallon Monday. Danny is really lucky to be on the Coral Sea. It is really very seldom that any of our carriers get down that way. I think they will be spending two weeks at Sidney. A couple gents from our Bass Lake excursion namely Howie Alexander roomed next door to me, and Ross Underhill are with VA-153 aboard the same boat.

Easter Sunday I had the duty but was invited to dinner by the Pearson's. Had to refuse though because you cannot leave the base when you have the duty.

You asked me a while back about Readers Digest. Yes I am receiving it and thank you again for it. Well that will be it for now. I will try to be more diligent in my correspondence.

Love,
Richard

26 MAY

Dear Mom & Dad,
    Well here I am back in Lemoore again for another week. We flew off the ship Fri. morning, flew a sandblown mission to a target near Yuma, Arizona, then returned to NAS. It wasn't too bad aboard for two weeks, although I was pretty tired. The week-end in San Diego was enjoyable also. I got 10 more carrier landings aboard the Midway (actually first-10 towards becoming a centurion on Midway - only 90 to go).

    When I got back Fri. I played a dance job at the 'O' club. Also have one Tues. nite.

    Sat. afternoon went up to Pine Flat Resevoir to go water skiing and swimming. The water was great and

RICHARD CHERBA

the sun was warm. (a little red on the forehead right now). This couple was camping out the week end and asked me to come up. He had killed a rattle snake a couple of hours before and at my suggestion we skinned it and had it along with our steak supper. It was delicious. Well I finally got home from there about 2 AM.

Sounds like you all have been keeping busy too, with the porch flooring, baking, etc. Also wish I were home to enjoy the glider. When I got back to Lemoore I had all sorts of mail including about 6 letters from you. They never did send any out to the ship.

No I won't be renting anything this summer at Bass Lake. We won't be

III around that much and not too many people have boats. Pearson's have invited me up when I can make it. Pine Flat is about 1:45 by car and Bass is 2:00 hrs.

As you may know the Pres. will be out this way the first week in June. On June 6 he will be on the U.S.S. Kittyhawk to watch operations and an air show. Our squadron has to send a bird for static display so I get to fly it down. Probably leave Thurs. nite as the plane has to be loaded aboard Fri. A.M. Then week-end liberty in San Diego. I will have to be aboard the entire week so I just may get to see or even meet him. Very slim chance! Anyway I probably won't have much to do that week.

Well I guess that brings you up to date on my activities. Have a nice Memorial Day and say hello to all.

Love,
Richard

1962

U.S. NAVAL AIR STATION
Lemoore, California

18 June

Dear Mom & Dad,

    First a very belated Happy Fathers' day to Dad. I'm sorry I didn't send a card but the ship didn't have any. Anyway your the best 'POP' in my book.

    Well I am fine and hope you are the same. Right now my left jaw is a little swollen. I now have 31 vice 32 teeth. One was extracted yesterday because the tooth had an abscess as a result from an old filling. The tooth gave me a lot of trouble about two weeks ago then the pain disappeared and I thought no more about it. Then it started to act up again and I went to the dentist. They took some x-rays and decided it should come out as soon as possible to save me pain later on. So out it came. Wasn't any problem at all.

Over the week end I played two dance jobs at Bass Lake. Stayed Friday night at the cabin (not renting it). Sat helped the Bearsons clean up the yard. Sun. I had the duty.

Getting pretty warm here — 106° yesterday —

Real nice living in an apt for a change. Finally getting everything straightened out.

I got to fly off the ship Friday. Was a pretty busy week. This next week end going on a cross country to San Diego.

I have a phone now — 582-3146 in Hanford.

We have today off so I think I will take a dip in the pool. Did you get the pictures.

Not too much else going on. So I'll close for now. Please say hello to Irene for me. I owe her so many letters she is going to disown me as a brother.

Love
Richard

U.S. NAVAL AIR STATION
Lemoore, California

22 July

Dear Mom & Dad,

I am fine and hope you are the same. Have been keeping busy with the squadron and then coming home to a beer, T.V. and bed.

Fallon was really a long deployment. We worked weird hours and a few days around the clock. On one week end we went camping and fishing. We went into the mts. about the 7-8 thousand ft level. It was a nice quiet two days. This was the Sat. & Sun. of 4 July. Thinking of going again this week end.

The first two weeks in Aug. we are going aboard ship again for some games. The 31 Aug. we head for Hawaii for 3 weeks.

I hope to take 8 days leave beginning 19 a.
I intend to drive up to Yellowstone Park
and camp along the way. It will be good to
get away for a few days and relax along
the way.
    Sat. nite we had a squadron
party at one of the officer's homes. He had steaks
of which everyone had to cook their own on the
barbecue pits. Everyone had some good chow,
a good time, and also a few drinks.
    Just got through watching a new
TV program called "Funny Funny Films", where people
show their home movies. It is almost as good
as candid camera. Sometimes I think that
some of the films that you have would
get a few laughs now and then.
    The aeroplane that I fly
is the A4C (Douglas "Skyhawk"). It
used to be the A4D-2N until they

changed the designations of the planes.

Played a dance job Friday at the O'club and also have one this Friday. Am playing with a couple of fellows from the base. One I used to play with in Pensacola. Three of us are officers and one is a civilian. We play the music we like and everyone else seems to enjoy it too.

Boy! H.N.Inc. has sure expanded from the one room that I used to know.

I see where Keefe Braselle is going to have his own show.

Listened to the Liston-Patterson fight for 2 min 10 sec. Patterson sounded like he didn't have a chance.

Well I'll close for now.

Love,
Richard

RICHARD CHERBA

> Hi, 19 AUG.
> Just a few lines to say hello. Got home Sat. night. It was a long 2½ weeks. Last night went to see "How the West was Won" in Cinerama. It was a very good picture.
> Leaving in a few minutes for Yellowstone via Yosemite and Salt Lake City so I will be writing from there. Then on the 30th will be heading for Hawaii for 3 wks. prob. 2 week ends in port. We will be in Hong Kong for Xmas this year. By for now!
> Love,
> Richard

August 19, 1963

Mr & Mrs John Cherba
2223 N. Ridge Rd.
Elyria 7
Ohio 44038

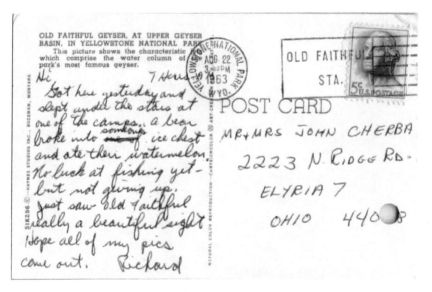

August 22, 1963

YELLOWSTONE PARK COMPANY
Lake Hotel
YELLOWSTONE NATIONAL PARK, WYOMING, 83020

23 AUG

Dear Mom & Dad,
    Just a few lines to say hello and that I am enjoying my few days here at Yellowstone.
    I stayed here tonight, it is right on Yellowstone Lake. The last two nights I slept out in my sleeping bag. This morning there was frost on the cars so it got pretty chilly. The park is only open one more week.
    Went horseback riding for an hr. this aft. Sure glad that was all!! I have seen all sizes & shapes of geysers. They really have a lot of them. Some (all) of the pools are also very beautiful with their

SIGHTSEEING TOURS · BOATING · FISHING and ISLAND FISH FRY · SADDLE HORSES
STAGECOACH RIDES and COOKOUTS · EXCURSION and SPEEDBOAT RIDES

various colors and formations.
Met several different people on vacation from Clev. & Avon Lake. Just about all of the help here is from out of state summer college students. It would have been nice to work out here one summer.

There sure is a lot to see here. I am leaving tomorrow, I have to be back on Wed. Did quite a bit of walking and am kind of tuckered out so I'll sign off for now. Haven't decided which way to go yet.

Mail future letters to VA-22 F PO SAN FRAN, CA I'll get them a tad sooner while I am on the boat. We are leaving on the 30th and get back on the 21st (SEP)

Bye for now —

Love,
Richard

RICHARD CHERBA

YELLOWSTONE PARK COMPANY
Lake Hotel
Yellowstone Park, Wyoming

Mr+Mrs. John Cherba
2223 N. Ridge Rd
Elyria 7
Ohio 44038

GRAND CANYON OF THE YELLOWSTONE
YELLOWSTONE NATIONAL PARK
AND THE 308-FOOT LOWER FALLS AS SEEN
FROM ARTIST POINT PRESENTS ONE OF THE
MOST IMPRESSIVE VIEWS OF THE GORGE,
WHICH THOMAS MORAN EXCLAIMED IS THE
MOST BRILLIANTLY COLORED LANDSCAPE
IN EXISTENCE.

POST CARD

PLACE STAMP HERE

3 SEP

Dear Mom & Dad,

I am fine and hope you are the same. Did you have a nice Labor Day week-end? I had the duty on Monday. Over the week-end I went to Bass Lake and water skied with some of Roger's friends. He was up there with me. We stayed at Pearson's Cabin.

Our voyage to Hawaii was postponed, but we will get back to there when we make our WesPac cruise in Nov.

On my way back from Yellowstone I stopped to see Barbara. She mentioned something about Johnnie G. running away from home for a few days. What's the story? Barb has been working all summer as a Kelly Girl. She'll be teaching 6th grade this year

I am trying to get home the end of Oct. or first of Nov. to bring my car home. If Irene or Gordon intend to drive it they will have to pay the additional fee for operators under 25, or else not drive it. I won't know

RICHARD CHERBA

until after Oct. 20. If I do I won't be able to spend much time at home as I will have to leave probably the day after I arrive.

Would you tell Aunt Grace that all men coming into the Navy have to do three months mess cooking. (Enlisted men) This is done before they are rated in a particular field, even though he has been to school.

This last week we received four shots. Typhus, smallpox, cholera, typhoid. They have a new way with an air gun. Really going modern! Arm was sore for a couple of days.

Too bad Dad had to make two trips to get a haircut. I thought it was funny.

Pictures of Brian are cute. He is really fat. Well I'll close for now. Will write again soon.

Love,
Richard

Attack Weapons Delivery Pilot Certificate

THIS IS TO CERTIFY THAT

LTJG R. J. CHERBA, USNR 644275/1315

having qualified in accordance with OPNAV INST. 03740.8 and COMNAVAIRPAC INST. 03401.3E, and having been recommended by his commanding officer as a pilot of marked competence and as a person of high integrity, is hereby designated an Attack Weapons Delivery Pilot in A4-C Skyhawk aircraft.

Done this 5th day of September 1963 at the Headquarters of Commander Fleet Air Alameda

D. J. WELSH
Signature and Seal

RICHARD CHERBA

30 OCT 63

Dear Mom + Dad,

I am fine except for a few sniffles. I hope all goes well with you. Ever since I came back from D.C. It has been go-go all the time. We flew off the ship Friday. I came home and played a dance job both Fri. and Sat. Sunday I caught up on my sleep that I had been missing. Monday I had the duty. Tuesday I worked and I had today off to get some of my gear squared away. Boy! do I have lot of junk that I have accumulated in the last three years. I am in the process of packing most of my gear for storage. I am taking all my uniforms and only a couple of suits with me. I would like to buy some things in Hong Kong.

We fly the airplanes to Alameda for loading aboard on Wed. 6th. I have the duty that day. So I will call home on the 7th between noon and 3pm E.S.T. The ship pulls out on the 8th

Have enjoyed living in the apt. Beats the drab BOQ anyday. Will give it up on the 5th.

I don't know if air mail will help. Your letters take about 5 days to get to me.

Just happen to think, what happened to G Vargo and that lawsuit?

Speaking of shots I had a yellow fever shot the other day which now makes a total of 7.

I have a few things, pictures, etc, that I will be sending home, also I will be sending home undeveloped film from time to time if I can't get it developed over there. If so let me know how they turn out.

Well I hope Gramma is feeling better and please say hello to everyone. I will call Thursday.

Love,
Richard

RICHARD CHERBA

9 Nov

Dear Mom + Dad,
    I am fine + hope you are the same. We left Alameda at 1000 Friday. It was raining, cloudy sort of a gloomy day. We had spent the night before in San Francisco, had dinner at Ernie's ($11.00 pp) and then proceeded to drink a few brews.

    As we began heading West, someone figured how many days it was until we pulled back in to Alameda, 200 exactly, today only 199.

    We get shore leave on the 16-17, 23-24 in Hawaii. We actually get in the area tomorrow or Mon. but we won't go into port but operate in the area for a while.

We flew a little today, just to practice Air refueling. I know have 48 landings aboard Midway (I have others on other carriers) which puts me halfway almost to becoming a Midway centurion. No special honor accorded except when you get 100 landings aboard one carrier, you can wear one more patch on your flight jacket.

Well I don't have to much more to say. I believe they are flying a load of mail to Oahu tomorrow, so I'll send this airmail just to see how long it takes. Bye for now.

Love,
Richard

RICHARD CHERBA

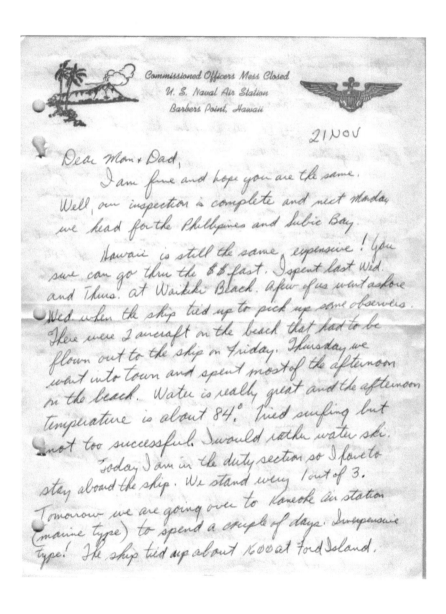

Commissioned Officers Mess Closed
U. S. Naval Air Station
Barbers Point, Hawaii

21 NOV

Dear Mom & Dad,
 I am fine and hope you are the same. Well, our inspection is complete and next Monday we head for the Phillipines and Subic Bay.

Hawaii is still the same, expensive! You sure can go thru the $$ fast. I spent last Wed. and Thurs. at Waikiki Beach. A few of us went ashore Wed when the ship tied up to pick up some observers. There were 2 aircraft on the beach that had to be flown out to the ship on Friday. Thursday we went into town and spent most of the afternoon on the beach. Water is really great and the afternoon temperature is about 84°. Tried surfing but not too successful. I would rather water ski.

Today I am in the duty section so I have to stay aboard the ship. We stand every 1 out of 3. Tomorow we are going over to Kaneohe air station (marine type) to spend a couple of days. Inexpensive type! The ship tied up about 1600 at Ford Island.

you can still see some of the sunken ships from 7 DEC '41. A lot of them have plaques on them and then of course there is the Arizona Memorial.

Yes, I do fly the Douglas Skyhawk. Its number-letter designation is A 4 C.

Your last letter was airmailed on the 18 and I received it on the 20th. Pretty fast service. We didn't get any mail on the way out. Only when we are within air distance to a port then a plane goes in and picks up our mail. When we are close like this for a couple of weeks our mail comes almost every day. The FPO at S.F. knows our movements so it sends mail to our next port of call.

I got the "Informer" from Rev. Bosco, plus 10 Nov program. There was a few lines on the "Inf." mainly, greetings plus a few additional remarks. He expects me home for Xmas, I guess! Lots of luck.

I believe Sonny lucked out and got shore duty where Danny got sea duty. Depends on what rate (job class) you are striking for.

The negatives I would like developed and the negatives returned to me.

Well, we have been keeping busy with General Quarters about 2-3 times a day + flying + studying various deals. Try to get some more letters off for now. Will write more next week for sure! Love Richard

RICHARD CHERBA

4 DEC 1963

Dear Mom & Dad,

Well I am fine and well and hope you are the same. The mail finally goes out tomorrow so I thought I had better jot down a few lines.

We haven't done any flying since we left Hawaii. The boat has just been steaming along towards the Phillipines. The weather has been very humid and hot. We will fly this Thurs. & Fri. and then pull in Sat. in Subic Bay until the 12, then to sea and pull into Hongkong on the 21-27.

Everybody is just tired of sitting around, although we all have our paperwork to catch up on. We have a movie in the ready room every nite and a lot of them have just been TV series. Some of them I haven't even seen. Talking about the heat before, our room (2 of us) is air conditioned so the nights are comfortable, so is the ready room.

As you can see by the menu, we had a pretty good dinner at Thanksgiving. We had it a day earlier than you did at home because we crossed the international date line, where we lost one day. We have set the clocks back several times to conform to the appropriate time zone that we are in.

While we were at Pearl Harbor my roomie and I (Hank Papa from Rhode Island) bought some goodies to have when we wanted. We have had tastes of smoked octupus, abalone, frog legs and of course the usual jam, crackers, candy, etc. All of it tastes pretty good, even the octupus. (Tastes like tough chicken)

Since we have had only one mail call since we left Pearl, I am looking for a lot of mail tomorrow just like everyone else. Bye for now.

Love
Richard

RICHARD CHERBA

11 DEC

Dear Mom + Dad,
 I am feeling fine and hope you are the same. We pulled in the ~~Philip~~ Philippines on the 7th. I had the duty. We have to stand every one day out of 3. That night I didn't feel good. I guess I caught the two day bug because I spent the next two days mostly in bed. So yesterday I felt a little better and went ashore and today I think I am back to normal.

 Hope you enjoy these postcards! I've seen a lot of this from the air, yesterday saw the island in a lake on an island in a lake on an island in the ocean. Confusing! Tried to see the active volcano but it was covered with clouds. You see a lot of fishing outriggers.

 Went into the city of Olongapo last night. I think it ~~~~ outdoes Tijuana in Mexico. Really not too much to talk about. We are going to be back here in January. Then will try

to get to Manila and Baguio, a summer resort here.
 Thank you for the money. I'll bring my gifts home with me as we can only send $10.00 max thru the mail duty free. At the end of the cruise I'll be able to bring it all home free.
 What color silk did Aunt Mary want and what kind + color do you and Irene want? I can get real good wooden objects here made of out of monkey pod wood. They have some nice salad bowls (sets) and of course they have the fork and spoon in all sizes to hang on your wall for decoration.
 We will probably see some snow in Japan. Talk about liquor, It is only about $1.50 a qt. for Beefeater's gin. We can take back about a gallon.
 Yes, it was a tragic thing about Pres. Kennedy. I'm sorry I even failed to mention it in my previous letter. The ship was anchored at Pearl Harbor and about 10 of us had gone over to the exchange (morning).

III. We passed thru the Radio-TV dept. and found a small crowd gathered around a radio. Of course what we heard we couldn't believe. Some of us stayed there for an hour or so before we left for the ship again. We here feel a great loss not only of a leader but as our Commander in Chief. I do feel that Johnson will be ever as good as Kennedy was.

Yes I can decifer the sizes. Will try to get some shirts made in Hong Kong. Any particular style, white, sport, short-long sleeve?

Your air mail letters arrive in about 5-7 days. Irene's 1st class mail takes about 9. Just info.

Bye for now. Going to try and water ski this afternoon. Try and get this in this afternoon's mail.

Hope you have a White Christmas!

Love
Richard.

December 25, 1963   page 1

The following 2 letters have been re-written because the originals are very hard to read and scan. They were written on Hong King Hilton paper, like onion skin. I think these are way better to read than the originals. I still have all of the material that my Mother kept and have used almost all of them.

We left the Philippines on December 13, 1963 on our way to Hong Kong. Where we arrived on Dec 21. 1963. Due to the ship's size, we had to anchor in the harbor and use a tender or one of the ships life boats to go ashore. About a 45 minute trip. While in port we had the duty for one day. The ship provided a small crew in one of these life boats to guard and repel any boarders of the ship at night. It had to have one officer that could command a ship (designated by a star on the uniform shoulder board), a chief and a very few sailors who actually ran the boat. The chief was the only person that had a side arm and could possibly repel intruders. This was a 4 hour watch and we just kept circling the ship. When our time was up, we were relieved by the next crew. I think I had the 12-4 am watch. While in port, the Chinese painted the exterior of the ship's hull. Dan Gildner and I hung out together and we did a lot of sight seeing.

RICHARD CHERBA

December 25, 1963 page 2

Dear Mom & Dad,

Well, a Merry Christmas! From the Hong Kong

Hilton. We are (Dan Gildner and myself) staying here tonight and maybe tomorrow night. Quite a fabulous place. It costs about 30.00 HK dollars or about $11.00 US for a room for two. HK is a shoppers' paradise. Especially on clothes. I'll tell you about it in my next letter which will probably tell you what I have been doing the last week or so. We have been doing a lot shopping and a lot of sightseeing. Had the duty the day before Xmas and went to church aboard ship that night.

The ship is anchored out so we have to catch a ferry every time we want to come in or bo back. It's about a 45 minute boat ride.

Tomorrow we decided to have breakfast in bed. Just for kicks! We act like the last of the big time spenders.

We leave here Saturday. And our section has the duty Friday so tomorrow is our last day in the city.

We'll be heading back towards the Philippines. Enjoyed all the Xmas cards and also look forward to your letters. Bye for now. Going out to dinner to improve eating Chinese dishes with chopsticks. Getting pretty good, too!

Love,

Richard

LETTERS

From Richard Cherba
to My Parents John & Irene Cherba
From US NAVY

1964

WINGS OF LEGACY

RICHARD CHERBA

12 JAN 1964

Dear Irene, Gordon, and Brian,

    Thought I would try out my new typewriter so please excuse the mistakes! Besides you can probably read this better than my handwriting.

    I am fine and hope everything goes well with you. I guess by now you have already read my letter about Honk Kong that I wrote to Mom & Dad so I won't repeat myself.

    The <u>day after</u> I left HK I received your letter about what type, color etc, material you wanted and I already have got it. So you should have written sooner. But I think that you will like what I picked out and if you don't you can give it to someone else. I'm not going to send anything home because I'm afraid that it will get lost. My room is beginning to look like a store with all the stuff that my roomie and I have bought. We even have some of our gear in another room. I bought two W70 Wharfedale speaker systems for 100.00 each and a Mirachord 10 changer for 92.00 (includes base and also legs for the speakers) The wood is teak and is unfinished. They really sound great.

    We arrived in the Philippines on 6 Jan and will leave on the 16th. The weather here is great. The squadron had a picnic last Wed. with beer, hamburgers, hot dogs, etc. The locations was Cubi Pt. Recreation Beach. We went swimming (some involuntaryly) and we also got some water skiing in. We played a couple of ball games too. The hours were from 1300 to 1800 and about 140 men were there. We drank some 35 cases of beer, 7 cases of soda, all totaled it cost us 108.00 for the whole deal. Chow was free from the ship.

    The squadron gave us a couple of days off so our duty section, 5 officers, went up to Baguio, a summer resort area in Northern Luzon, about a 5 hour journey by car. We left a 0800 in the AM and got there about two. What a beautiful place and there were some outstanding homes that belong to some millionaires in Manila. The drive was interesting. We saw how most of the people work and live. It is really surprising to note that most of the people speak some English. I guess it is taught in all the schools.

II
That night we did what all good Naval Aviators do and that is visit all the bars and see some floor shows. The following morning we played 18 holes of golf, I shot 100, fairly good for not having played for about 7 months. That afternoon we went into the village where they make all the hand carved wooden objects out of monkey pod, and mahogany. I bought some things here also. We had to leave that afternoon. We went up in a Special Services car and it costs us total 17.50 driver and all. Sure glad that I didn't have to drive the roads here are paved but are in poor shape! At night people drive their pony carts right on the road, most of them without lights. Some of them are even pulled with water buffalo.

Flying over the Islands is a kick in itself. I have seen Bataan where the battle was fought. You can still see the caves, gun emplacements, and fort all aged with the years and probably would have a good story to tell if they could talk. There are also "kraals" (I think) many of them. Aren't they used to capture fish? Seems to me that I remember studying them in school. The water is so clear around some of the Islands that the view makes you want to go down and live on a desert isle.

Our next port of call is Sasebo on the island of Kyushu of the Japan chain. We will be there from the 24-30.

If there is anything in particular that you would like please let me know. DO NOT Repeat DO NOT Send any money.

Boy Santa Really took care of Brian! I'll be bringing his gift home also.

Oh, You mentioned something about china. Sned(send) me a picture of the kind you want and I will see if I can get it for you also glassware. They have some good buys in Japan. So write now and not after I leave there!!!!!

Well I guess that's about all for now. Give Brian a kiss for me and I'll write again soon.

Love,
Richard

15 January

Dear Mom & Dad,

I am fine and hope you both are feeling better.

Thought I had better tell you that I finally received the cookies and most of them were still in one or two pieces. But, BOY ARE THEY GOOD!!!

The xmas card you forwarded was from Carol and Ed Logue. They now live in Northvale, N.J.

The letter I sent home didn't cost me 2.00. The way the mail works is that from the ship the mail goes by air (if at sea) to the nearest port and then by gov't air back to the U.S. THEN it goes according to the postage. The same works in reverse. But mail is always by air to us from the U.S.

I'll say right now that please don't send me *anything* for my Birthday!

Our trip up to Baguio was interesting in many ways. Irene's letter has all the good dope. I really enjoyed playing on their golf course and also buying some wooden objects. The people were very good.

How is the sale of the house going? I hate not to go back to that place.

Well I can't think of anything else so I'll close for now.

Love,
Richard

RICHARD CHERBA

21 JAN 65

Dear Mom + Dad,

I am fine and hope you are the same. Sorry about not writing sooner.
Thank you for the money, I can use it to pay some of my bills and also the license. I took the exam and passed it on the 31 DEC. That afternoon I rented an airplane (Cessna 172) and 4 of us flew to Las Vegas for New Years (2 days). We really had a good time.

We were supposed to go to sea on the 18th but it was postponed. So we leave tomorrow for Alameda and the ship leaves Mon. A.M. until 5 FEB with us aboard for operation off the coast of Southern California. We will be back for two weeks and then again leave on the 22nd for another 2 weeks. We will pull in for a couple of days and then on 6 MARCH leave for WestPac.

It doesn't look like I will be able to get home at all now. The CO doesn't want birds stranded all over the U.S. just before we go to sea.

This last week-end I went up to

I Sacramento to see Barbara. We had a pretty wild week-end. Her roommate is a nut too!

Glad to hear the the loan went thru for Irene & Gordon.

Abie, one of my former roomies here at the house got married two weeks ago. So now Skip and I are here now. Fray was here for about 3 weeks. Still hasn't found a job. (He really isn't looking either.)

Not too much else to report right now, so I will close. Bye for now —

Love,
Richard

23 Jan.

Dear Mom & Dad,

    I am fine and hope that the cold winter is not too uncomfortable. We, too, have moved further north and temperatures are in the 50's. In fact the water temp. is warmer (64°) than the air.

    We now have to wear our anti-exposure suits for protection against the water, etc. if we should happen to eject. They are made out of rubber and are water tight (I hope!). They are sort of uncomfortable as the rubber fits like a glove around the neck and wrists. The boots are attached which also are water proof.

    Sometimes when we have manned our aircraft on the flight deck, it has been raining, snowing or sleet. The weather really has been cold.

'yes I would like those negatives back eventually. No hurry though!'

I don't know why you want a 3 bedroom home. I should think that a 2 bedroom would be sufficient.

Well tomorrow we pull in to Sasebo for seven days out of which I will get 4 days to look around. We will be getting further North also as the cruise goes on. Beppu, Iwakuni, Yokosuka and Kobe. I might go to Nagasaki, where they dropped the A bomb. I understand it has been made into a memorial. But I'll tell you about my trip after I've been there.

It was the owners that took us out to dinner in H.K. The tailors themselves we never saw, but were told that they have a union and apprentice

RICHARD CHERBA

I program, just like everybody else. The shoe shop was the same way, however, they took us to the basement where they had about 30 employees making shoes. It was very interesting to see how they did it.

I bought a Nikkoax camera for $29.95 in the Phil. They say they are worth $130.00 in the U.S. It's not really fancy but it has a few more gadgets that my Kodak didn't have, and I paid 30.00 for it (KODAK)

I got a letter from Ray Pauluk the other day. He wants me to start a music store with him when and if I get out. He now lives in Concord, Calif, just outside of San F. Ray has a pretty good head for figures and says that the area is really short of good teachers. I'll have to give this some serious consideration. I wouldn't mind trying a business, especially one I would enjoy.

Well I guess I better get back to work. We have been flying on a long schedule ever since we left the Phil.

Before I forget let me say now: "Happy Anniversary" on your 28th Wedding Anniversary. I pray that you have many, many more.

Love,
Richard

RICHARD CHERBA

30 Jan.

Dear Mom & Dad,

I am fine and hope you are the same.

Tomorrow we leave Sasebo and spend 12 days at sea. Then we anchor off Beppu for 3 days and then move over to Iwakuni for 3.

My first two days were spent very well. We had a change of command for the skipper of the ship in the afternoon. After this we took our first trip into Japan. We got a hotel room for the night. It was in a typical Japanese setting. We slept on the floor, actually on a heavy thick quilt, with a few heavy pieces on top for a cover. It was very comfortable. The hotel had the sliding doors and straw mats, and they even gave us some welcome tea.

Sunday at noon we took a 1½ hour express train to Nagasaki for some sightseeing. We saw where the A bomb fell. It really is amazing how the city has built up since then, of course it has been almost 20 years.

Most of the people have turned to Western style dressing. The old people still wear the traditional Japanese dress including sandals.

We had a TAXI take us around and you can see the route on the enclosed pamphlet. The museum is quite interesting as it has various curios about the bomb and how various objects were fuzed together plus a lot of pictures.

The statue of peace is a huge monument dedicated to peace. It is made out of bronze.

RICHARD CHERBA

After the tour, we just walked through the stores, again finding most of them open in front. They have no heating, but they have a pot which is very warm that everyone stands around when they aren't busy.

We caught the last train (9:12) back to Saseba, because we had the duty the next day. This wasn't the express, but a 2½ hr. deal. The trains run on time without fail. They are very dependable. The countryside has a lot of farmland, mostly rice paddies.

The 28th we went to a Japanese restaurant for dinner. The menu was beef sukyaki (SOO-KIYA'KEY) and boy was it delicious. They cook it right at the table and of course no silver just chopsticks. You sit on the floor, legs folded. They cook it in a pot about 17" in diameter. Beef, onions, bean cake, lettuce, cabbage, corn etc. all cooked together. You dip some in raw egg and then ~~go~~ take some cooked rice and gum gum!

Afterwards (incidently the 5 of us were all in one room) a geisha girl came in and entertained us with games done with matches. We all were drinking saki. She was very pleasant and everyone had a good time.

That is Sasebo in a nutshell, except for the normal amount of alcohol intake, everyone had a good time.

Thank you for my birthday gift. If the china is the set I bought you I believe I remember the pattern. I'll wait until I get to Yokosuka before I get it.

We ~~two~~ leave for Continental U.S. on 16 MAY from Subic Bay, Phill. Islands. It will be about a 10-15 day crossover.

RICHARD CHERBA

How is the house deal coming? I hope it is successful.

On 1 Mar. I become the Communications Officer. They squadron is switching a few jobs around and mine is one. The idea is to broaden our scope in various jobs. It will give us a better idea of what goes on in other departments. I'm ready for a change anyway.

Well, I'll close for now until next time.

Love
Richard

24 February 1964

Dear Mom and Dad,

I am fine and hope you are the same. I trust you will find this letter more of a pleasure to read than my familiar "Redcock" scratch.

The last seven days have been at sea with two more days to go. Wed. five of us will fly into Atsugi a Naval Air Station on the island of Honshu. This will be for five days of operations (shore-based) and then 2½ days of liberty when I expect to go to Tokyo and see the largest city in the world. I then come back to the ship for 2½ of duty then two½ days of liberty where I intend to try to take to the mountains and some skiing -I Hope. The reports that the lodges are all booked up. And of course if my finances hold out. And then back to the ship for 2½ more days of duty. We leave Yokosuka on the 12 of Feb. The ship will tie up at Yoko for some upkeep repairs while the squadrons will send various deployments to Atsugi for operations.

At sea not a whole lot happens except that we do a lot of flying and watch movies when we have time. Since the ship received a new Captain, Sundays have been a complete holiday routine and we haven't had to work. In the past we had Holiday routine until noon and then flight ops until 2200 or later. Sunday we watched three movies all day long and just relaxed. During the week we usually operate from about 1000 until 2200. In fact on Sundays Special Services runs Bingo games.

On the 12 of Feb we pulled into Beppu for 3 days then to Iwakuni. for 3. Beppu is a Japanese resort town which doesn't have alot to see except fountains and spas similiar to those of Yellowstone. There is a long tram that takes you to the top of a mountain, which is very breathtaking and exciting. This is in Iwakuni.

Iwakuni is nothing but a series of "stand-up bars". I did make a side trip to Hiroshima by train. Takes about an hour and cost about 1100 US. It was really interesting to note the comparison between Hiroshima and Nagasaki. The re-building and all. They have a very good museum and have pictures of the area soon after the blast. It really wiped out the city. But it sure doesn't look like it now. They did let one structure stand as a sort of Remembrance to all of what happened.

While in the park my friend and I were stopped by several girls who were in junior high school who just wanted to talk with us. I guess they just wanted to practice their English. They spoke very good English however they had a hard time understanding our questions. They even took our autographs and our pictures. A very interesting experience.

Just happened to be reading all the talk about the World's Fair. I sure would like to attend it sometime next fall. Maybe it could be around Dad's vacation and we could go together if it could be worked out and you wanted to go. Besides I sure would like a chance to drive that new OLDS. WOOOOOOOWWWWWWWWW!!!!!!!!!!!!!!! FIRST CLASS. It sounds and is priced like a real fine auto. Looking forward toward the first photo of of that you can spare.

Haven't as yet filed my income tax. At present I have it figured that I will get back about $X 127 or so .

Well my typing is getting worse so I'll close for now and write again from Atsugi and Toyko. Say hello to Gramma and everyone for me. Bye for now.

Love,
Richard

RICHARD CHERBA

14 March 1964

Dear Mom and Dad,
I am fine and hope you are the same. Well we are at sea again and have a little more time to catch up on my mail. When the boat pulls into port I like to make maximum use of all the liberty I can get.

We flew off the ship on the 26 Feb to NAS Atsugi about 1 hour and ¥ 170 away from Tokyo. We stayed there for 5 days and flew local missions. Got to see a lot of Japan from the air and the snow covered mountains are really beautiful. We flew over some ski resorts and saw a few people skiing. Of course, we also have flown over and around Mt. Fuji-san (Fujiama) and have taken many pictures of it from the air. Most of them came out pretty good. I am mailing my pictures in film mailers to PaloAlto, Calif. and getting them back in 8-10 days which is pretty godd service.

Dan and I spent two rainy days (no pictures) in Tokyo. Stayed at a military hotel Called the Sanno for $3.80 a night. We went to the Mikado and the Kabuki Theater which we enjoyed very much. I wrote Irene a couple of days ago so I am probably repeating myself.

I checked on the China and they don't make that pattern anymore. I am going to call the factory in Tokyo next time we are in Yokosuka. They do have some shakers that would go good with your set, they are plain. Would you want these? Also Irene has some patterns to choose from for dishes and if you want any please let me know prior to 1 Apr.

We spent most of our time and money at Atsugi. It was pleasant to get away from the ship for a while.

When I have the duty this means that 1/3 of the ship's company must be on board at all times. we are split up into three duty sections. so every third day we have the duty day. This last time in port when we went to Atsugi to fly this was adjusted a bit and we sometimes had to stay aboard for 1-2½ days, which isn't bad since we get to go away on side trips for two days at a time.

Just received the enclosed picture. The skipper had a growth removed from his hose and had to wear a band-aid. So the following morning at quarters all the officers showed up with band-aids on our noses. Everyone got a big laugh out of it especially the skipper and his boss who is also a Commander (three stripes). Then we came to the ready room and this photo taken. The TV set that you see in the picture is called PLAT- Pilot Landing Aid Television. It records on tape all landings and take-offs and shows them back when you come back from a hop to view your techniques and mistakes.

About the film. They don't sell 16mm aboard ship and I haven't checked yet in the exchanges.

Enjoyed the picture of you and Brian on your Anniversary. You both look real good and Brian sure is getting bigger.

Haven't figured my income tax out completely but I'll get some back this year.

Saw an interesting sight yesterday. We flew over a live Volcano that had erupted a few days ago. It looked like you were seeeing clearly down to hell and you could actually see the red molten lava burning. Ie ven said hello to the devil. Any way it was an unusual sight that you quite often don't see.

Would you say again the dates of Dad's vacation and possible iternary? I have forgotten what it was.

Well I will close for now and try to write again soon. Life at sea is always the same routine and it very seldom changes.

Love Richard

3. April 1964

Dear Mom & Dad,

    I am fine and hope you are the same. We left Yokosuka on the 31 of Mar. We didn't go to Kobe like we had anticipated. We did some additional flying from Atsugi.

    I was very sorry to hear about Johnny Y. I didn't get a card but I did write hime a short letter. I hope he is getting along better. Ol' Doug McArthur reminds me of Gramma. Except he is a little more in worse shape. Gramma is doing well and I hope that she still is.

    Thank you very much for the Easter Card and gift. I hope that you too had a nice and enjoyable Easter.

    I have taken up the game of golf and have even purchased a set of clubs. I got the bag, complete set of clubs, and covers for the woods all for 96.00. The shoes are going to cost me about $9.00. It is sort of a good way to relax and exercise off the ship. They have a winter 18-hole course at Atsugi that I have played several times.

    On April Fool's Day I got my 100th landing aboard Midway. Quite a few of the pilots from the air wing are getting them about the same time. My total are now about 104 aboard Midway. Starting towards 200, but probably won't make until next cruise, which will begin next February.

    I have not put in for any leave when we get back around the end of May but will take it later in the summer around Aug. or Sep. Our Squadron hopes to have about one cross country a month for each pilot so I am going to try to take one to Dayton for a week end in July. I can take a bus home from there.

    Well not too much else for now. Have to get ready for a hop and get some lunch. Chow is still pretty good.

                                 Love
                                  Richard

RICHARD CHERBA

22 APR 64

Dear Mom + Dad,
 I am fine and hope you are the same. Our schedule is changing so much that we sometimes don't know what we will be doing next.
 The ship is still the same, still the daily routine. We anchored out of Sasebo for a few days and I played some golf. Haven't been doing to much sight-seeing. Our period up in Yoko was really miserable for liberty. It rained just about every day and Japan isn't exactly made for "Walkin' in the Rain." So I didn't go anywhere and I neverever broke out my camera.
 The picture was taken in Yoko by a gent in the squadron and he gave it to me. I just happen to be going forward to my room, which is near the starboard catapult. We were tied up there as you can see the little hill next to the pier
 Sasebo is our last stop in Japan from here we head towards the Phillipines. And leave Cubi Pt. around the 12th MAY for San Francisco. Everybody is ready to go home, Days to Alameda is **35**. I've enjoyed myself and wouldn't mind being stationed over here for a couple of years. The buys over

here are really tremendous. I think my money was spent wisely and that I really didn't throw it on any junk. There is a lot of that, too.

Today we received a message from Commander Naval Air Pacific saying that our Squadron was awarded the Battle Efficiency Award. It entitles us to paint 'E's on our aircraft and wear appropriate markings on the uniforms. (enlisted only) The was for the 1962-64 cycle. The award means that we are the "Best A4C Squadron in the West." (west coast) and there are 18 of them. Our inspection grades, competitive exercises, and individual 'E's (of which I have 3 — about average) all added up to make us the Top "Skyhawk" attack squadron in the Pacific Fleet. Needless to say we are all proud of the fact. We are the only ones on the ship that received it.

I did have a choice as to when I took leave. I figured I would have a little more capital in Aug. I hope to take about 2 weeks then and another week at Xmas. I would like to spend about a week at home and then spend a couple of days at the Fair in N.Y.

I'll close for now and write some more later.

love,
Richard

ORDER OF PROTESTANT WORSHIP
26 April 1964
ORGAN PRELUDE
THE CALL TO WORSHIP
*THE HYMN: "Blessed Assurance"   No. 164
INVOCATION
THE AFFIRMATION OF FAITH:
            THE APOSTLES' CREED

I believe in God the Father Almighty, maker of Heaven and Earth; and in Jesus Christ His only Son, our Lord; who was conceived by the Holy Ghost; born of the Virgin Mary, suffered under Pontius Pilate, was crucified, dead and buried; He descended into Hell; the third day He rose again from the dead; He ascended into Heaven and sitteth on the right hand of God the Father Almighty; from thence He shall come to judge the quick and the dead. I believe in the Holy Ghost; the Holy Catholic Church; the Communion of Saints; the forgiveness of sins; the resurrection of the body; and the life everlasting. Amen.

*THE RESPONSIVE READING: "The House of God"   No. 479
*THE GLORIA PATRI: No. 420
NOTICES AND GREETINGS
SCRIPTURE LESSON: Revelation 3:7-13

THE PASTORAL PRAYER AND THE LORD'S PRAYER
*THE HYMN: "Onward, Christian Soldiers"   No. 289
SERMON: "An Opportunity"   Chaplain Lawson
*HYMN: "Eternal Father" (V. 1,4)   No. 399
*BENEDICTION
ORGAN POSTLUDE

              *Indicates Congregation Standing

You are invited to join us for the Vesper Service in Memorial Chapel at 1900 hours today.

              WHY PEOPLE GO TO CHURCH

        Some go to church to take a walk;
        Some go to church to laugh and talk;
        Some go there to meet a friend;
        Some go there their time to spend;
        Some go there to meet a lover;
        Some go there a fault to cover;
        Some go there for speculation;
        Some go there for observation;
        Some go there to doze and nod;
        The wise go there to worship God.

                USS MIDWAY (CVA-41)

Captain W. WRIGHT, USN   Commanding Officer
CDR D. H. STINEMATES, USN   Executive Officer
LCDR M. A. LAWSON, CHC, USN   Chaplain
R. K. BERNHAGEN, PN3, USNR   Chaplain's Assistant
A. E. FIORE, SN, USNR   Chaplain's Assistant
D. A. CHAMBERS, SN, USNR   Chaplain's Assistant

ATTACK SQUADRON TWENTY-TWO
c/o Fleet Post Office
San Francisco, California
(96601)

27 April 1964

From: Commanding Officer, Attack Squadron TWENTY-TWO
To: Attack Squadron TWENTY-TWO

Subj: Battle Efficiency Award

1. The following messages have been received by the squadron concerning our winning the COMNAVAIRPAC "E" for light jet attack squadrons:

"FM COMNAVAIRPAC
TO ANYNAVAIRPAC

UNCLAS
NAVAIRPAC BATTLE EFFICIENCY AWARD WINNERS 1962 - 1964 COMPETITIVE CYCLE.
A. CNAVINST 3590.4A
1. IAW REF A THE FOLLOWING NAVAIRPAC SQUADRONS ARE AWARDED BATTLE EFFICIENCY PENNANTS FOR 1962 - 1964 COMPETITIVE CYCLE:
    VF(F-4) - FITRON 143   VA(F) - ATKRON 115   VP'S - PATRON 40
    VF(F-8) - FITRON 191   VAH - HATRON 2   VS - AIRANTISUBCOMTWELVE
    VA(J) - ATKRON 22   GP(J) - LATWW 4   HS - HELANTISUBRON 2
2. COMPETITION AMONG SQUADRONS IN ROUTINE WAS EXTREMELY KEEN. ALL UNITS CAN BE JUSTIFIABLY PROUD OF THEIR ACHIEVEMENTS. TO ALL AWARD WINNERS CONGRATULATIONS AND WELL DONE. VADM P. D. STROOP."

"FM COMFAIRALAMEDA
TO ATKRON TWO TWO

NAVAIRPAC BATTLE EFFICIENCY AWARD WINNER
A. COMNAVAIRPAC 21 00022 (NOTAL)
1. ACKNOWLEDGEMENT THAT YOU STAND NUMBER ONE AFTER SIXTEEN MONTHS OF COMPETITION WITH ALL OTHER VA SQUADRONS IS A GRATIFYING MOMENT FOR YOU. THE AREAS COVERED BY THIS COMPETITION ENCOMPASS MANY VALUES, ALL POINTED TOWARD COMBAT READINESS. MY PERSONAL OBSERVATION OF YOUR SQUADRONS SHOWED SOUND ORGANIZATION AND DEDICATION TO THE IDEALS FOR WHICH WE STAND IN TODAY'S NAVY. YOUR EXAMPLE OF LEADERSHIP IS HIGHLY COMMENDABLE. COMFAIRALAMEDA ADDS HIS CONGRATULATIONS TO EACH AND EVERY MEMBER OF YOUR TEAM."

"FM USS KITTY HAWK
TO ATKRON TWO TWO

UNCLAS
RENOWNED VA-112 BRONCO SENDS HEARTFELT CONGRATS TO VA 22 REDCOCKS. WE ARE POOR LOSERS. BEWARE THIS CYCLE."

"FM COMSEVENTHFLT
TO ATKRON 22

UNCLAS
NAVAIRPAC BATTLE EFFICIENCY AWARD
1. I WISH TO EXTEND MY HEARTIEST CONGRATULATIONS TO THE OFFICERS AND ENLISTED MEN OF ATKRON 22 ON THEIR ACHIEVEMENTS IN WINNING THE BATTLE EFFICIENCY AWARD FOR THE 1962 - 1964 COMPETITIVE CYCLE. THIS OUTSTANDING ACHIEVEMENT REFLECTS THE SUPERB LEADERSHIP, SUPERVISION AND SUPERIOR TECHNICAL SKILL OF ALL MEMBERS OF YOUR COMMAND. THIS FEAT IS INDICATIVE OF WHAT TEAMWORK AND AIRMANSHIP, PLUS DEVOTION AND SPIRIT AMONG PROFESSIONALS CAN ACCOMPLISH. WELL DONE. VICE ADMIRAL MOORER."

2. Many of you have asked about the various items considered in making the award. Basically they are as follows:

   a. Competitive Exercises (COMPEXS) we conducted at Lemoore and Fallon. Our marks on these exercises were based on pilot performance and how well our aircraft and ordnance systems functioned once airborne.

   b. Operational Readiness Inspection (ORI).

   c. Safety programs and overall Safety record.

   d. Grades received on Administrative, Material and Maintenance Inspections.

   e. Such other areas as may be stipulated by the type commander.

3. As you can see from the various items considered that it included almost every phase of squadron performance. Winning this award could not have been accomplished without the tireless efforts and skills of each member of the squadron. I extend my wholehearted congratulations and a well done to each of you.

R. S. SMITH

3 May 1964

Dear Mom & Dad,

I am fine and hope you are the same. The weather has really warmed up and we are in short sleeve shirts again. This is only because we have returned to the area of the Philippine Islands. We will operate around here until we pull into Subic Bay on the 9th. The temps aboard are not too high as yet but I understand that the temps at Cubi Pt. are in the high 90's. I like warm weather anyway.

Again I missed getting a card but I want to wish Mom a very happy Mother's Day- and hope that the day is bright and cheerful for you.

The enclosed picture was taken in the ready room the other day by a poloriod camera. All in the picture flipped a coin to see who would win the picture and I won. The gent in the white jersey is my roomie Hank Papa. The others are all in the squadron also, most of them sporting our new ball caps that we purchased in Yokosuka. Thought you might enjoy looking at the programs. I didn't go to church hardly at all at the beginning of the cruise but have been trying lately to make a special effort to go at least every other Sunday. The Chaplain isn't a great speaker but I feel that I have to go to make my life complete.

The other letter is from the Skipper on our winning the 'E' from Commander Naval Air Forces Pacific Fleet.

Eleven will get to fly off the ship a day early on the 26th to return the aircraft to Lemoore. Haven't decided whether or not I will live off base as yet. Have to wait to find out if I will be able to draw an allowance for quarters. This amounts to $95.10 a month extra. I got it last summer and I don't anticipate any delay this year.

How is the new car running?

Alson enclosed find an announcement about Zoller's new baby girl. Heard from Ben Book the other day. He is studying as the University of Arizona at Tuscon. Terry is expecting sometime this month. May be able to get down there by air if I can to say hello.

That is it for now, will write again soon.

Love,

Richard

RICHARD CHERBA

11 MAY

Dear Mom + Dad,
 Just a few lines to say hello before the mail goes for the last time from WestPac. We leave Cubi (cubi) pt. at 1400 today.
 We will be going home the great circle route which takes us North close to the Aleutian Islands. This is a shorter route. We may or may not operate (fly) on the way back.
 I got the negatives in good Shape.
 Sat. afternoon we had another picnic on the beach, played ball, drank beer, and ate some hamburgers and hot dogs and a few steaks.
 It isn't too hot here, there has been a nice ocean breeze to keep the air circulating. Spent yesterday playing 9 holes of golf and swimming at the pool.

Well as I say sayonara to the West and hello West I close for now and write when I get back to Lemoore.

Love,
Richard

---

13 May 1964

Dear Mom & Dad,
    Just a few lines to say hello and that I am fine. Well we are finally on our way home. We left the Philippines on the 11th at 1407. We are doing a little flying on the way home but not very much.
    I have put in for a cross country to Patterson AFB at Dayton. If it gets approved I will leave Lemoore on 8 Jun and get there around 3 or 4 in the afternoon and would leave on the 10th early in the am. Henry Papa will come with me. I won't know for a while until I get back to Lemoore whether or not it will go through. I hope it does and that way I will get to see you all before Aug.
    Have you heard anything about the property deal yet? They are sure taking there time.
    We are going home the Northern route so we will not stop in Hawaii. Returning ships seldom go through the islands on there return home.
    What is Aunt Julia's address? I may be able to get out there and see her sometime this summer.
    As for the 'E', the competition runs 16 months. Our competitions, individual 'E's at Fallon. I believe I am repeating myself.
    Does Dad know when his vacation will be and have you decided where you are going?
    Just read Life's maga-ine on the Fair. Looks like a fantastic place. Really would like to see it.
    12 more days until the fly off. YAHOO!!!!!!!!!!!
    Will close for now for lack of any more writing material. Hope to see you in June. Bye for now.

LOVE,
Richard

RICHARD CHERBA

16 June '64

Dear Mom & Dad,
    I am fine and hope you are the same. Sorry to be so long in writing, but the following will explain: Our trip to Olathe, Kansas was uneventful and so was our trip to Alberquique, N.M. We flew some lo-level from Kansas to N.M. The land sure is flat and rolling. A lot of farms. After fueling and filing our flight plan, we turned up and then my aircraft went down because of a loss of the fuel boost pump. They didn't have any on the station so Henry went to Lemoore and returned the next day with a replacement. I stayed at Dave & Kay Hill's apt. (former squadron mates) also had dinner there. Got back to Lemoore Friday at 7 pm. (10 pm your time) and went to Happy Hour. Found out from Bob Frazier, my roomie from Phoenix, Ariz. (other is Dave Abrahamsen) that he had found a 3 bed-room house for 150.00 mo. in Lemoore. So we spent the whole week end moving in. So far I still haven't put everything away but

have got most of the essentials. The place was really filthy so we had a cleaning job to do before we unpacked anything. The place really looks homey, we have pictures & figures & all sorts of jazz all over that we purchased in WestPac. We have living "stereo" — 4 units of speakers - loud man loud!!! set up in our living room. It sure beats the BOQ.

Just in case you should have to reach me my phone at work is: 209-998-3260
home: 209-924-4423
address: 40 LINDA LANE
LEMOORE, CALIF.

but continue to use squadron address.

We have 4 planes: "Princess" with light in my bedroom.

I still have some gifts to send home when I can get to them. Probably by mail.

Not much else for now. I enjoyed being home again very much and Henry really liked the chow. Looking forward to coming home again soon.

Love,
Richard

RICHARD CHERBA

24 June 1964

Dear Mr. & Mrs. Cherba,

    I want to thank you both very much for the wonderful stay I had in the great state of Ohio. I can honestly say the hospitality shown to me was like being in my own home.

    I have asked my wife to attempt to cook stuff cabbage and I am hoping it turns out as good as yours. It better come close because Dick will most likely be over to eat it good or bad.

    Here's wishing this little note finds you all in the best of health. I again say THANK-YOU for the wonderful time.

                  Respectfully,

                    Henry Papa

June 27, 1964

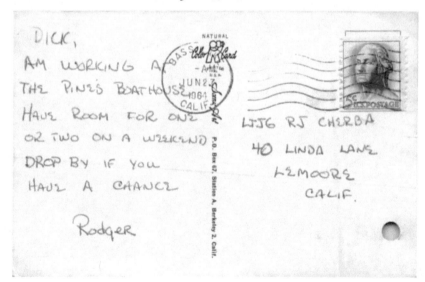

RICHARD CHERBA

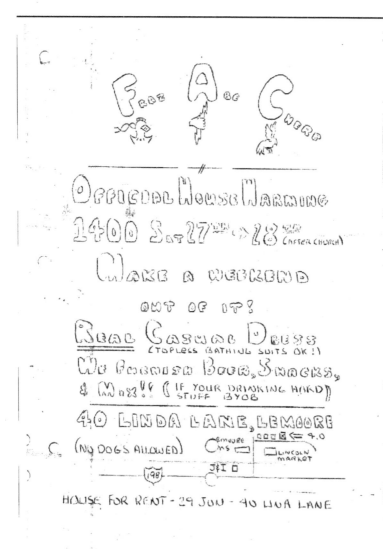

Line reads, "We Furnish Beer Snacks & Mix !!"

WINGS OF LEGACY

In June 1964, there were three of us that became real good friends and we decided to rent a three bedroom house $150.00/mo in Lemoore. Bob Frazier was in VA-23 Our sister A4 squadron, Dave Abrahamsen VA-25, an AD Spad A/C.Propeller driven. And me, VA-22, A-4. We usually were not there at the same time due to our schedules. We decided to have an open house. We had shirts made for each of us.

Bob would become my best man for our wedding. We decided to throw a house warming party and left these flyers everywhere. We had a 'uniform' made for the party so that people would know who the hosts were. We also had a huge sign, blue with the white letters that we put on the roof of the house facing the street. Didn't want anyone to miss the party! The letters read-FAC, Fraz, Abe and Cherb. We had a blast and the party lasted into the wee hours. 3 AM.

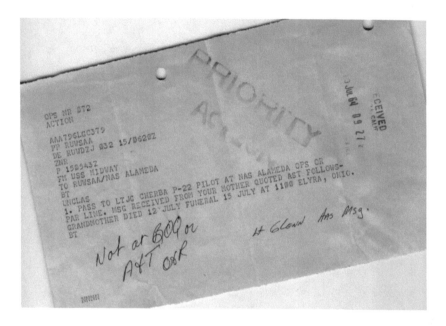

11 July

Dear Mom + Dad,

I am fine and hope you are the same. I want to say again that I did enjoy being home for a while and also the little pup Brian. He really is a hand changer.

We finally had our house warming on the 27-28 June. WOW!! what a weekend! Sat. night we must have had 150 people over. It was a B.Y.O.B. affair. We hired a bartender for 11 hours, and he mixed all the drinks. I finally went to bed about 5 AM Sun. and there were still people dancing in the living room.

Needless to say the house was a complete wreck that AM. Bob (Fehr's) mother + aunt had driven up from Phoenix for the affair and by the time we woke up (about 11 AM) they had the place just about cleaned up. Boy were we ever grateful.

Sunday the party continued on and we finally closed down about Mon. 3 AM. All in all it was a real great weekend.

The 4th of July 4 couples and two of us bachelors rented the house and sleeping porch up at Bass Lake. We also had a good time, skiing, swimming and dancing and drinking at the Falls at night.

We are at sea again until the 17th. We left Alameda on the 8th. Just normal refresher carrier ops. It seems as though we never left this non work.

I hope everything at home is coming along, will close for now have to fly in a couple of hours.

Love,
Richard

16 July

Dear Mom & Dad,
   Please accept my deepest sympathy in the loss of your Mother and my Grandmother this past week. Please also express my thoughts to everyone else at home as I doubt that I will write to everyone. I am sorry I could not have made the funeral but I guess we had thought this over before and thought it best that I need not be home although I do wish that I could have been there.

   I received the message about 1000 PDT (1:00 EDT your time) on the 15th. The day before I left the ship via cod off the coast of San Diego to depart to Alameda to pick up a bird that had completed Par and that we needed aboard ship. I went into San F. that night and got home about 2 AM. The C.O. passed the message to Alameda as soon as they received aboard Midway. The people at Alameda called the BOQ several times but each time the steward claimed I wasn't registered, which I had been since the night before at 8pm. So as I walked in to file my flight plan they gave me the message.
   I then called home and talked to Dad. He said everyone is OK, except Brian with the chicken Pox.

II. Where did he get those? I'm sorry that Mom wasn't home when I called. Right after I called I had to return to the ship. We will fly off tomorrow morning. The mail leaves the ship at nine so I had better get this letter down there. Air Ops were cancelled this AM. Bad weather.
I have put in for leave from 24 AUG to 6 SEP. Hasn't been approved as yet. Will keep you informed.

With all my love,
your son,
Richard

WINGS OF LEGACY

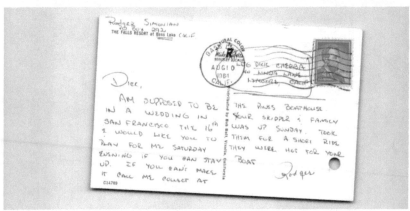

August 10, 1964

RICHARD CHERBA

3 Sep.

Dear Mom & Dad,

    I arrived safely here at Lemoore. The meal and cocktails were fairly good and there weren't too many people on the plane. I stayed at a motel that night and caught the 7:05 to Visalia.

    Enclosed are the Hawaii fares and another brochure. Self explanatory. Presently packing for Fallon, will head for the lake this afternoon. Not too much else for now.

                  Love
                    Richard

9 Sep.

Dear Mom + Dad,
 I am fine and hope you are the same.
 I left for the lake on Thurs. AM and got back Mon. night. It was a pleasant week-end and a long one. I stayed at Rodger's apt. and slept in my sleeping bag. The boat is running fine. It is now in our garage as I brought it out Mon.
 My hay fever is completely cleared up. It doesn't bother me too much out here, only late at night when there is a lot of dust in the air. Otherwise I hardly ever use a handkerchief.
 This AM we flew to Fallon so I thought I would drop a line. I have the duty today.

RICHARD CHERBA

Everybody is in town tonight trying their luck. If anybody has any $ left we will go to Reno this week-end. There are about 4 or 5 cars up here that some of the people drove up. Some of the guys even sent their Hondas up on the gear truck. We will be leaving here on the 25th.

Well not too much else to tell, so I'll close for now.

Love,
Richard

15 SEP

Dear Mom + Dad,
I am fine and hope you are the same. We are still at Fallon and the work is running smoothly. The weather here has been nice, a tad cool in the evenings.

The picture is of the 5th lobster we had in Rhode Island (and me of course). It has been in my flight suit all this time and I am finally washing it.

We spent a real nice weekend in Reno. All of us had dinner and stayed overnight at the Holiday Lodge about 5 miles West of Reno. The chow was great. For #4 I had prime rib that was 1½" thick and very large, really outstanding.

A couple of us met the owner and he loaned us a couple

RICHARD CHERBA

II of bathing suits and at sunset we were swimming in one pool 80° fed by mineral water and another 85°. It was really great. We also saw a brief show Sun. evening at the Primadonna in Reno.

Not too much else. Here is Paul Yuresko's address and you might give the subscription blank to Irene, its free and interesting paper.

PAUL YURESKO
3110 N. 46th PLACE
PHOENIX 18,
ARIZONA

Bye for now.

Love,
Richard

13 Oct

Dear Mom + Dad,

I am fine and hope you are the same and had a nice cross-country trip.

I hope the house was clean when you arrived, as Jack & Carol may have told you we had another big party (about 100 or so people) the Sat. before we left. We left the keys with a cleaning woman and hope she cleaned the house.

We have been operating since Sun. and will tie up at Pearl for one day on the 15th and then out to sea and then in on the 21st for four days prior our return to Conus.

We will tie up for 1 night at NAS North Island in San Diego on either the 28 or 29th before going back to sea again off of the coast and pull into San Francisco on the 6th or 7th. Probably will be home on the 7th for sure. (Nov.)

RICHARD CHERBA

1. The fork & spoon are on my bed. Please take them will you. I hope to see you if you are able to stick around Pensacola for awhile but I know that you might want to leave to don't feel bad if you don't get to see me. The Navy had other plans.

Will write again soon, must get dressed for dinner.

Love,
Richard

21 Oct.

Dear Mom + Dad,
 Just a short note to say hello. Everything is going fine out here. Hawaii is expensive as usual.
 The ship will be at NAS North Island on the 28 & 29th of Nov. If you're not going to remain in Lemoore maybe I can see you then, if not won't be home until the 7th. Noel is at San Diego.
 Hope you are enjoying your trip. Will close for now and catch a few Z's.

            Love,
            Richard

RICHARD CHERBA

15 DEC

Dear Mom + Dad,

I am fine and hope you are the same.

The valley is in its fog condition again and our flying has been very limited.

I won't be in Dayton this week end. Am going to try in Jan. and also try to leave on a Thursday so that I will be able to spend more than one day in Ohio.

This last weekend Bill Neuman and myself flew to Luke AFB in Phoenix to see Fray my former roommate. We left Sat. and started back Sun. but the weather at Lemoore was socked in so we diverted to Alameda and returned to Lemoore Monday aft.

Today I have the duty. Also have the duty on Xmas eve. This will make three in a row for me. Oh well! Will probably have Xmas dinner at the Papa's.

Still haven't decided what to do with my 7 days leave over New Years. Maybe I'll just stay home and loaf for awhile.

I took a physical a few weeks ago. It was required as part of my application for augmentation. This will also serve as my annual. The only thing wrong was a few cavities and maybe the removal of a molar that seems to be in the way. Looks like I'll lose another one.

If your home on Xmas day about 3p.m. your time I call home.

Still haven't bought cards yet. Guess I'd better get going.

Well to bed for me. Oh yes received the 'goodies' in good shape. Haven't seen the neighbors yet to find out if they got theirs. They why are outstanding as you can bake them.

Give my love to all!

Love,
Rickard

RICHARD CHERBA

1964
20 DEC

Dear Mom + Dad,
    Hope you had a nice Christmas and lots of snow. I am feeling fine and hope everyone at home is well also.
    We left the Philippines on 13 Dec. and have been operating around the islands all week. Tomorrow we pull into Hong Kong. Everybody is quite anxious to get in and spend their money. This is a free port of the British Crown Colony and consequently many purchases can be made very cheaply, even cheaper than in the original country.
    Aunt Mary sent me $5 for 3 yds of material. So I'll get enough for her with the $25 you sent. Thank you very much for my Xmas gift and I'm looking forward to the goodies. Some of the fellows received goodies, those that arrived in fair condition were those in coffee cans.
    Irene sent me $5 also for Xmas.

I really would like to get them something nice. Value makes no difference. Do you know what they'd like?

Enclosed find some more stamps. I am also saving various kinds of money. In the Philippines the rate of exchange was $5.00 = 19.85 pesos. I have some folding money in addition to some change.

Well I started this letter awhile back, today is 3 Jan. and I hope you had a nice New Years! Sorry, I have been neglecting my letters. Hong Kong was really great! The first day we went in and shopped for a good tailor. I had a summer suit, winter sport coat, couple pair of slacks and some shirts made. We had about 3 fittings thruout the week and picked them up on our last day in port.

The next day the tailors took us on tour of the new territory, (Barry, Dan, and Myself)

RICHARD CHERBA

III. We saw the refugees from Red China stacked up on the slopes elbow to elbow. Really bad.

Hong Kong is in two parts. There is H.K. Island and then the Kowloon Peninsula. Most of our time was spent on the Kowloon side. Easily traversed by the Star Ferry for only 10¢ H.K. By the way $1.00 U.S. is equal to $5.70 H.K.

On the tour we also saw the border of Red China from a viewing point of about 2 miles.

We only had 4 days in H.K. (Had duty on the other days.). The 3rd day we took a H.K. island tour, which included lunch on a floating restaurant at Aberdeen. see (Post card). Here you can actually pick the fish you want to eat, They are all alive. We then stopped at the Peak tram, which is a railroad that goes straight up a hill, and also the famous Tiger Balm Gardens. A sort of Disneyland with no moving parts.

It has beautifully painted scenes of the chinese people, ways etc. I guess the kids really get a kick out of it.

That night we went to dinner at the Princess Gardens and an eleven course meal, paid for by the tailors again. There were about 13 of us altogether. As you can see by the menu, we had some pretty interesting courses, and I tried all of them. These were Pekingnese? dishes. By this time all of us were becoming pretty adept at using chopsticks and I got to be pretty good. I can't even remember using a fork.

Dan and I spent two nights at the H.K. Hilton. By the way did you get a letter from there. What a place that is!! Really good service! We had breakfast in our room. The rooms (military rates) cost us $30 HK apiece or about $5.50 U.S.

(5) It was a lot more convenient to stay there than commute back and forth to the ship with a 45 min. ferry ride, because the ship was anchored in the harbor.

We left H.K. on noon of the 27th and are now operating around the Philippines again. We pull in Monday 6th thru the 15th to operate ashore and then operate and head for Sasebo, Japan.

Still haven't received the goodies yet. It takes some pkg. a month to get here. The letters have more of a priority. We sometimes get 1500# of mail by aircraft which lands aboard. So you see there is quite a lot.

I hope Gramma is feeling better. I'll have to drop her a note and say hello.

Sure hate to see you move from the castle but I guess it's just too big for you and Dad.

I bought an Olympia typewriter so I will try to type my future letters. Maybe you'll be able to read them. It is the Olympia SM 7 and I paid 395.00 H.K. or about 69.00 for it. Check and see what they run at home.

We can only send packages of $10.00 value or less duty free. So I will bring the silks when I come home. Besides I hate to think that they might get lost or stolen.

Well I think I have brought you up to date so far. So I'll close out for now.

love,
Richard

P.S. I guess I forgot to tell you the best news of all which I heard on Xmas day. My name appeared on the Lieutenant selectee list that recently came out. I can't put on the "railroad tracks" ("Lieutenant Bars") until I get my letter which will probably be next Nov. I have to have 4 yrs. commissioned service in and my original date of comm. was 21 Oct 60 so it will be somewhere around Nov. All (4 of us) that were elgible in the squadron made it. Bye for Richard

LETTERS

**From Richard Cherba
to My Parents John & Irene Cherba
From US NAVY**

1965

21 JAN 65

Dear Mom + Dad,

I am fine and hope you are the same. Sorry about not writing sooner. Thank you for the money, I can use it to pay some of my bills and also the license. I took the exam and passed it on the 31 DEC. That afternoon I rented an airplane (Cessna 172) and 4 of us flew to Las Vegas for New-Years (2 days). We really had a good time.

We were supposed to go to sea on the 18th but it was postponed. So we leave tomorrow for Alameda and the ship leaves Mon. A.M. until 5 FEB with us aboard for operation off the coast of Southern California. We will be back for two weeks and then again leave on the 22nd for another 2 weeks. We will pull in for a couple of days and then on 6 MARCH leave for WestPac.

It doesn't look like I will be able to get home at all now. The CO doesn't want birds stranded all over the U.S. just before we go to sea.

This last week-end I went up to

RICHARD CHERBA

I ---

Sacramento to see Barbara. We had a pretty wild week-end. Her room mate is a riot too!

Glad to hear the the loan went thru for Irene & Gordon.

Abe, one of my former roomies here at the house got married two weeks ago. So now Skip and I are here now. Fray was here for about 3 weeks. Still hasn't found a job. (He really isn't looking either.)

Not too much else to report right now, so I will close. Bye for now —

Love,
Richard

29 JAN

Dear Mom + Dad,
 Received your card + letter today. Thank you. As my usual stupid move I forgot to buy a card but anyway a Very Happy Anniversary and may you both enjoy the years to come.
 We are still at Sea. Left Alameda Monday morning after a pretty good week end spent in S Fran. Just as we pulled out into the channel after passing under the Golden Gate, a Greek freighter just about ran into us. It was a pretty close call.
 We have been working long hours again. Yesterday 18 today 15.
 Gee Whiz sounds like everyone has Pneumonia at home. Is it that cold? I am fine. Had a sore throat for about a day but a couple of lozenges fixed it right up.
 I think maybe I will get out and look around for awhile in May. Applied for a job with TWA Haven't heard from them yet. Oh well I still can't make up my mind Well close for now. How is June doing?
 Love,
 Richard

RICHARD CHERBA

23 FEB 65

Dear Mom & Dad,
    Just a few lines to say hello and that I am fine. Hope you are too.
    We flew aboard ship today and will be back in Alameda on the 3,4,5 MAR. Leave the 6th for Hawaii. Will try to call before I leave.
    Am sending some pictures and a magazine (we are on the front cover). There are some slides and an undeveloped roll of film that I haven't the faintest idea of what is on it. Be careful you don't discard something.
    Finally got everything put away and moved out of the house.
    The boat is at 415 E. 7th Street, Hanford GARAGE.
    The stereo & drums at Jack & Carols, 30 LINDA LN. LEMOORE
    The TV at CHIC & MAY STILES 995 LAUREL LN LEMOORE
    and the rest of my stuff, golf clubs, clothes etc at 40 LINCOLN in the garage packed in cartons.
    The car is at Foreign Automotive in Hanford on 10th AVE. being fixed up & painted.

    By the way to you have a Power of Attorney for me. If not I'll get you one in case something should happen.

Well will close for now. Give my love to all. When is Irene due?

Love,
Richard

ALOHA!   19 MAR

Hi,
    Just a few lines to say hello and that I am fine. Hope your colds are over with.
    We pulled into Pearl Harbor yesterday afternoon. We had left last Monday AM for our O.R.I. I haven't heard the results yet but I guess we did all right. Everyone on the whole ship gets graded. It sure was great to get it over with. We must have went to General Quarters about 3-4 times daily. Of course we did a lot of flying too.
    Hank Papa, Warren Lee and myself are hitching a ride tonight in a Navy beechcraft and going over to the island of Kauai. The

II "Garden Island." It is the neighboring isle to the West of Oahu about 80 miles. It will be something different to do, I'm rather tired of Waikiki and Honolulu. The plane will pick us up Sunday PM and return us to Barbers PT. They say that the island is the most beautiful of all.

The ship pulls out Mon. AM for the WEST. We were scheduled to go to Yokosuka for 5 days but now we are going direct to Cubi. PT. (Philippine Islands). So it looks like we will be involved in the situation over there. In addition there isn't too much in port time scheduled, so we will be spending long periods at sea.

No I am not actually in one of those AIRCRAFT on the front cover. It is our squadron though and we do this everyday.

Well bye for now. Next letter probably from Cubi.

love,
Richard

Lumahai Beach 3/22/65

I was the butt of a practical joke, Fun, but frustrating.

I was assigned a refresher in the ship for a

simulator period. Time came and off I went to find it among the ship's compartment numbering systems, very complicated. Nobody could tell me where it was. I was close but could never figure it out, until someone suggested that they were playing a joke on me.

We did something similar in High School for new neophytes that were in plays. Props were stored in the school attic and we would sent them up there to get 2 sky hooks.!! I should have known that you could not use a simulator on an wavy ocean going vessel.

U.S.S. MIDWAY
CVA-41

24 MAR 65

Dear Mom + Dad,

Just a few lines to say hello and hope everyone at home is well. We are just steaming along. The weather has been nice and we have daily meetings on various subjects to help pass the time. We will arrive the first part of April.

Just to fill you in on a few things that could happen out here I want you to ~~know~~ be aware of them as it could happen to me. We have to be realistic so please try and not to worry. Everything will turn out all right.

First if I should happen to become a P.O.W. in Viet Nam (or anywhere for that matter) and I am alive and well, we will be allowed to correspond through the Red Cross in Geneva. My letters will indicate only that I am OK and more than likely will be rather cold. The Reds will screen these and of course extract any info they can get from the letter to use on me. So only expect to hear about my death and nothing else.   3-24-65

    The other situation of course is death, and if it happens, well it was meant to be. I have seen many people die for no reason and if it is my turn, God willed it that way and I'm sure you both (Irene, too) will understand.

    In either case, a Red Cross Representative or someone from the Navy will contact you personally to assist in any matters that you may have. You can depend on him to be very helpful.

    It is just about certain that we will be flying some strikes into Viet Nam so that is what we have been training for. Other squadrons have been there before us and others will be there after we leave. It is just g something that has to be done.

    On to a lighter subject. We really had a great time on the island of Kauai. We rented a car and drove just about on every road there is to drive on. Sat AM. we drove to the Waimea Canyon (similar to the Grand C.), a little disappointing because the fog had come in and we really didn't see too much. That afternoon we lay on the beach it and went for a dip. In the evenings we just sat around and sipped our toddies and sang songs. There were quite a few older people there. Sun AM we played 18 holes of golf on a course right next to the ocean, really beautiful. We even rented an electric golf cart. (BIG SPENDERS) That afternoon we drove up the Northern side close to where South Pacific was filmed. The island was very beautiful and we really enjoyed the relaxed spirit of the isle as compared to OAHU and Waikiki. Sun. evening our former skipper CDR ABBOTT came for us in a Navy Beechcraft and took us home. Needless to say we were rather beat!

    This letter is probably coming from Hawaii. It is going back on the oiler that is topping us off tomorrow. Well will close for now and please don't worry.

Love,
Richard

3.24.65

U.S.S. Midway CVA-41

Happy Birthday — Pop!
Many Happy returns of the day
May you live to be one hundred
Sorry I didn't get a card but I hope this will do.
       Love,
         your son,
           Richard

U.S.S. MIDWAY CVA-41

9 APR

Dear Mom + Dad,

I am fine and hope you are the same. We left Cubi yesterday afternoon and are proceeding west. We should be on the line tonight at midnight. And I guess we can expect to see some actual combat anytime after that.

Having some film developed that I took on Kauai and having them sent directly home. Hope they turn out. If I didn't say before I did receive the check + the candy, both for which I thank you very much. The candy was shared with the people that happened to be around at the time I opened the box.

Sorry to hear about Gordon's Grandma. I don't believe I ever met her.

I Haven't seen my orders yet. Don't know what is holding them up unless this Pan Am strike is. I believe they do a lot of mail runs for the Gov't. Anyway I can not leave the squadron until I see them.

The pictures Hank took on Kauai. The car is a VW that we rented. The observation tower is the canyon but as you see it was a bit foggy.

Well until my next letter I will close for now.

Love,
Richard

April 8, 1965

Monarch Of The Carrier Dailies

MID-WATCH

Friday, 16 April 1965

NEWS GATHERED BY WEATHER SERVICE OFFICE AND RADIO ONE
PUBLISHED BY THE U.S.S. MIDWAY PUBLIC INFORMATION OFFICE

AIR STRIKES TO
BE STEPPED UP

TOP OF THE NEWS

STRIKES TO BE STEPPED UP

WASHINGTON, April 14 (UPI) - American air attacks on Red North Viet Nam will be stepped up in an effort to persuade the Hanoi regime to accept President Johnson's proposal for "unconditional" peace talks, officials here said Wednesday.

They reported that the United States does not consider Hanoi's initial rejection of Johnson's suggestion as necessarily being the final word from the Communist leaders.

As U.S. air attacks destroy more and more communications and installations, President Ho Chi Minh and his colleagues may well decide to count their losses and agree to talks, these sources declared.

Johnson is sending Henry Cabot Lodge, former U.S. Ambassador to Saigon, on a six-nation Far Eastern trip to discuss Viet Nam with "leaders of important friendly governments". Lodge plans to leave this week.

An elaboration of the revised U.S. "carrot and stick" strategy in Southeast Asia also is being given editors and broadcasters from throughout the United States in a two-day series of background talks here.

Defense Secretary Robert S. McNamara, Secretary Ball and State Department counselor Walt W. Rustow were on the schedule as today's speakers. Yesterday, Secretary of State Dean Rusk, William P. Bundy, Assistant Secretary of State for Far East Affairs, and a dozen other officials talked to the newsmen and answered their questions.

The speakers disclosed, among other things, the administration's conviction that it is extremely unlikely that Red China will intervene with ground forces in the Viet Nam conflict.

They also underlined what they considered differing reactions in Peking and Hanoi to the President's April 7 Baltimore speech on peace talks. They said they found some indications that the North Vietnamese and Red China were not taking exactly the same tack.

Meanwhile Peking argued against Johnson's suggestions in some detail and took issue with him on specific points, the Hanoi reaction was less categorical, they asserted. U.S. officials said that North Viet Nam had simply given an almost automatic but generalized rebuff but left the way open for reversing itself if conditions warranted.

-MORE-

STRIKES TO BE STEPPED UP CONT.

Hanoi came back with its own extremely general suggestions. It called for a return to the 1954 Geneva agreement guaranteeing the independence of individual parts of what was formerly French Indo-China, with all foreign troops pulled out of the area.

The American view that Red China is not likely to intervene on the ground in Southeast Asia within the foreseeable future seems to be based on two considerations:
— Red China did not intervene in Korea, even when the U.S. forces crossed the 38th parallel, until the Communist North Korean government had been driven so far north that it appeared on the verge of oblivion.
— There is little justification for Chinese troops when North Viet Nam already has a 250,000-man military machine which could be quickly employed if Hanoi decided to enter the ground struggle in the south.

U.S. officials acknowledge that if this latter event occurs, it would require revision of current strategy and possibly bring about an introduction of large-scale American ground forces.

RUSS-SINO GAP OVER V.N. WIDENS

LONDON, (UPI) - The Soviet-Chinese rift over Viet Nam was reported today to be widening sharply with increasing Peking suspicion that Moscow was scheming to establish a firm foothold in Hanoi.

Diplomatic reports said that Peking continues to keep close watch on Russian arms supplies to North Viet Nam for fear that Soviet experts and military men might accompany them and establish themselves in Hanoi.

Russians proceding to North Vietnam, via Red China were understood confined to fly on specified routes and by night, apparently to guard against Soviet "spying."

Relations between Peking and Moscow were authoritatively said to be "almost hostile" in regard to everything concerning Viet Nam.

The Communist Chinese, after prolonged negotiations, have finally allowed Russian arms supplies, notably anti-aircraft rockets to pass through their territory to North Viet Nam.

But diplomatic reports said the Chinese are keeping a close watch on all consignments and require detailed specifications. In the past they stopped some consignments and examined them closely for reasons of their own, the reports said.

The reports said there was increasing evidence that Russian rockets have reached North Viet Nam, though their type and numbers are not known. Nor is it quite clear who operates them, the North Vietnamese having little, if any experience with this type of weapon.

SUKARNO WEDS 17 YEAR OLD

KUALA LUMPUR (UPI) - Indonesian President Sukarno has taken his fifth wife, a 17-year-old beauty from West Java, the Malay Mail reported yesterday.

The newspaper, quoting an unnamed European executive who had just come from Jakarta, said the marriage took place two weeks ago but has been kept secret.

The girl was described as coming from a humble Javanese family.

If true, the Indonesian President is still within Moslem law which allows four wives. He divorced his first wife in 1942 when she failed to bear him an heir. Since then he has married Fatmawati, Hartini and a Japanese girl.

BRITISH AIRLINER CRASHES

ST. HELIER, CHANNEL ISLANDS (AP) - A British airliner crashed in fog on the island of Jersey Wednesday night, killing 23 passengers, most of them French and Italian, and three of its crew.
The airline said the only survivor was Dominique Silleere, 23-year-old air hostess from Paris.
The twin-engine DC3 plunged into a new plowed field short of the St. Helier runway. It had taken off from Paris with French and Italian hotel workers coming to Jersey for the Easter vacation season.
EDITOR'S NOTE: UPI reported only 22 passengers killed.

RUSSIA'S 'GOLD' LADIES

MOSCOW (UPI) - Soviet authorities have smashed a ring of gold speculators who used their profits for vodka, caviar and drunken orgies, it was reported Wednesday.
Two of the gold black marketeers, both women, were sent to prison.
One of them, Sara Khaliullina nicknamed "Queen of the Banknotes" amassed 22 pounds of gold and engaged in dirty parties."
Maria Tugush, the other, forced her daughter, Larissa, to confer her favors on foreigners to get gold. Maria had a weakness for caviar and pleated skirts.
Pravda did not say how long their prison sentences were.
Another member of the ring was a 70-year-old woman who stuffed gold coins into a mattress with her "palsied fingers."
The ring bought gold, mostly coins, from Russians and foreigners and sold it to "bigger and bigger fish."
Small fry in the gold market, nicknamed "mug," "small mug" and "hillbilly" bought the precious metal from Russians in front of a state gold buying shop.
A big fish, according to Moscow Pravda, was Ali Bagirov, from Baku.
Most of the gold, the newspaper indicated was bought and sold up the ladder for profits until it reached Bagirov's greedy hands.
The only prison sentences announced were those for Maria and Queen of Banknotes. The other apparently are still awaiting trial.

PEACE CORPS TO LEAVE

WASHINGTON (AP) - The United States and Indonesia have agreed "that in light of the current situation the U.S. Peace Corps should cease operations in Indonesia," a joint communique said Wednesday.
The statement issued at the conclusion of talks between special U.S. Ambassador Ellsworth Bunker representing U.S. President Lyndon Johnson and Indonesian President Sukarno also announced a cutback of U.S. economic assistance to Indonesia.
The joint statement said Sukarno and Bunker recognized that differences over Malaysia policy have produced tensions between Indonesia and the United States.
The statement added that "as a result, the programs of assistance to Indonesia which the U.S. has undertaken in recent years should be reviewed and revised on a continuing basis to be sure that they conform to the desires of the two governments."

54 MILLION MILE DATA RECEIVED

WASHINGTON (UPI) - Mars-bound Mariner 4, the National Aeronautics and Space Administration (NASA) deep space explorer, set a communications record Wednesday for U.S. spacecraft.

It transmitted scientific and engineering data back to earth from more than 54 million miles in space. Shortly after 9 a.m. EST Mariner 4 exceeded the previous record of 53.9 million miles set by Mariner 2 which flew by Venus Dec. 14, 1962.

Contact with Mariner 2 was lost on the 129th day of its flight, Jan. 3, 1963 after it had travelled 19 days beyond Venus. Today is the 137th day in space for Mariner 4 and it has 91 more to go before its closest approach to Mars July 14.

U.S. LAUNCHES BIGGEST STRIKE

SAIGON, April 15 (UPI) - Aircraft from all four American armed services teamed up today for the biggest air raid ever launched against Communist guerrillas in South Viet Nam.

An American Air Force spokesman said a combination of 230 aircraft bombed from dawn to dusk a Viet Cong stronghold northwest of Saigon.

The raiders included rocket and machinegun firing, U.S. Army helicopters and planes from the Air Force, Navy and Marines.

The airplanes rained 1,000 tons of bombs into a Communist stronghold 65 miles northwest of Saigon.

The explosives shattered a forested target area less than four miles long and two miles wide.

It was the first saturation bombing ever carried out against a Viet Cong hideout.

The raid was described to newsmen by Lt. Col. Jean K. Woodyard, 43, of Newark, Ohio.

Woodyard is Deputy Director of American air operations in South Viet Nam. He said today's raid was ordered last week by Gen. William C. Westmoreland, the Commander of American forces in this country.

Woodyard said that the target was the zone the Communists have nicknamed Duong Minh Chau, after a long-dead, guerrilla hero.

The impenetrable patch of forest in Tay Ninh province has long been suspected to hide the supreme headquarters of the rebel movement.

U.S. STUDIES RED MOTIVES

WASHINGTON (UPI) - The State Department is studying North Viet Nam's recent peace proposals, not so much for what they said but to fathom the motives behind them.

The details of the four-point proposals, announced Tuesday under the name of North Vietnamese premier Pham Van Dong, were plainly unacceptable to the United States.

But the fact that the statement was made was of considerable diplomatic interest. Both Washington and Hanoi have now put on the public record their conceptions of the ingredients of peace.

President Johnson gave his in an April 7 policy speech at Baltimore and an April 8 reply to 17 neutral nations who had called for peace negotiations.

VIET JUNK FLEET
TO REGULAR NAVY

SAIGON (UPI) - South Vietnamese Prime Minister Phan Huy Quai has signed a decree that will bring South Viet Nam's unorthodox junk fleet into the navy as a regular unit.

The decree, signed Wednesday, will become effective in July, according to the official Viet Nam press agency.

The junks have operated in the past as a paramilitary organization. The crews are paid to fight the Viet Cong and harrass Viet Cong shipping.

After induction into the regular navy the junk fleet sailors will be given regular ranks and receive the same pay and benefits of the Vietnamese Navy sailors.

The junk fleet sailors at present wear the black pajama-like clothes of the Vietnamese peasant. Their boats are armed with light machine guns.

The junk fleet operates with U.S. Navy advisors.

FLOOD IN H.K.
ON MALAYSIAN $

HONG KONG (UPI) - For the past two weeks there has been a flurry of purchases of Malaysian dollars in Hong Kong, and speculations were that Indonesian President Sukarno is behind it in connection with his economic war against Malaysia.

Indications show that the Chinese Communist banks are not the main buyers.

Malaysian dollars can be bought legally in Hong Kong market, so long as the buyers offer enough.

INDIAN FORETELLS
1970 EAST-WEST WAR

MANILA (UPI) - A visiting Indian astrologer who claimed he predicted President Kennedy's "calamity" in 1963, today forecast an East-West war sparked by Communist China in 1970.

Shastri Revashanker Baradwala, a 57-year-old Indian Swami, made the prediction when he visited the editorial office of the Manila Daily Mirror this morning.

"I chart the future by looking at the stars," he said in a published interview. "For instance there are no astral signs that there will be war up to 1970. By 1970, however, planets Saturn and Mars will be very close as though they are on a collision course.

"Although there will be war in 1970, the Philippines will not be involved because the Philippines is neither East or West and the coming war will be between the East and the West. It will be Red China that will make trouble."

Baradwala said he had predicted the victory of Philippine President Diosdado Macapagal in the 1961 elections, a "calamity" for President Kennedy in 1963 and the collapse of the Tokyo summit talks last year among the Philippines, Indonesia and Malaysia.

AMBASSADOR TAYLOR'S
SISTER-IN-LAW KILLED

PHILADELPHIA (UPI) - A 35-year-old woman shot and killed the sister-in-law of Gen. Maxwell D. Taylor Wednesday in what police described as a "mercy slaying" and then drove to Bethesda, Maryland, where she took her own life in front of a police station.

The slain woman was Mary Happer of Bethesda, 61-year-old sister of Mrs. Lydia Gardner Happer Taylor, wife of the U.S. Ambassador to South Viet Nam.

U.S. STUDIES RED MOTIVES CONT.

Johnson's formula: The United States was prepared for "unconditional discussions." But any settlement must involve an end to Hanoi's infiltration, supply and direction of the war, an independent South Viet Nam and adequate guarantees against resumed aggression.

Hanoi's formula appeared to be: The United States must stop bombing the North; it must withdraw from South Viet Nam; the South Vietnamese must settle directly with the Viet Cong guerrillas "in accordance with the program" of the Viet Cong; pending "peaceful reunification," both North and South Viet Nam would exist "without foreign interference" or alliances.

"If this basis is recognized," Hanoi said, "favorable conditions will be created for the peaceful settlement of the Viet Nam problem and it will be possible to consider the reconvening of an international conference..."

North Viet Nam said nothing directly about the points in Johnson's formula.

The whole exchange got precisely nowhere. But it posed a question: Was Hanoi's statement meant as a flat rebuff or as a counter-proposal?

If the Reds entertained any thoughts of eventual negotiations, they would still hardly jump to embrace Johnson's proposals.

To some readers, the statement lacked the quality of stark rejection found in recent pronouncements from Peking. The United States has generally pinned what hopes it has had for a negotiated settlement on the fact that North Viet Nam may not be a complete satellite of Red China's militancy, but may also have interests aligned with Russia and interests of its own.

WILSON ADDRESSES 1900 BUSINESSMEN

NEW YORK (UPI) - British Prime Minister Harold Wilson Wednesday night pledged to save the pound sterling and outlined his government's economic program which, when completed would "knock the hell out" of American competition.

Wilson addressed the Economic Club of New York in an hour-long expose of the labor government's program.

"Given the response of which our people are capable, be under no illusions we shall be able to knock the hell out of you," he told 1900 top U.S. businessmen at the Waldorf Astoria. They responded to the challenge with warm applause and laughter.

MINNESOTA FLOODED

CHICAGO (AP) - The swollen Mississippi river spread havoc across Minnesota lowlands Wednesday and threatened scores of communities in its path downstream.

Melting snow and ice pushed the Mississippi and its tributaries over their banks in Minnesota, Wisconsin, Iowa, North Dakota and Illinois, central American states.

U.S. President Lyndon Johnson inspected the flood and tornado-stricken region on foot and by plane and promised that government disaster relief funds to help the devastated communities would be forthcoming.

The latest reports of the number killed in a series of Palm Sunday tornadoes showed 130 dead in Indiana, 54 in Ohio, 46 in Michigan, seven in Illinois and three in Wisconsin, a total of 240.

The spreading flood already has forced an estimated 31,000 persons to leave their homes and caused damage in excess of an estimated 20 million dollars in Minnesota alone.

At least 11 deaths in Minnesota have been blamed on the floods.

KILLING CONT.

She was shot to death in her room at a nursing home in historic Germantown following a ride with her slayer through the springtime countryside.

Her "best friend," Mrs. Dorothy Butts of Bethesda, jammed what appeared to be the pistol used to kill the woman into her handbag and fled the home. She dashed across a terrace to a parking lot and sped off in a light-colored automobile.

In the excitement, officials at the High Oaks home for Christian Scientists did not report the slaying to police immediately.

It was more than an hour before police learned the details and telephoned an alarm to Bethesda authorities. Bethesda police went to Mrs. Butts' home but found no one home.

Shortly before 11 p.m. two officers entering the Bethesda police station saw the light colored automobile described in the Philadelphia police report.

They looked inside and found the body of Mrs. Butts, a .22-caliber bullet in her head.

A note found on her body at Suburban hospital told the story in one heart-breaking sentence:

"Today, I killed my best friend, Mary Happer, of 7305 River Rd., Bethesda, Maryland, who has been suffering so cruelly from cancer."

KOREAN STUDENTS BATTLE POLICE

SEOUL, SOUTH KOREA (UPI) - University and high school students battled Seoul police in the streets for the third straight day today, and 20 trucks loaded with Army troops moved in to protect the Central Government building.

President Park Chung Hee hurriedly called in Premier Chung Il Kwon, Defense Minister Kim Sung Eun and Home Minister Yang Chan Woo for conferences on the rising tide of demonstrations against the government.

The students are protesting the expected signing of a basic treaty settling old grudges between Korea and Japan.

Over 3,000 students fought police in the streets today--and for the first time their ranks included black-uniformed high school students.

Some 1,500 school boys from Kyungi high school marched off their campus but were driven back by the tear gas grenades and swinging clubs of police.

Thirty-three of the high school boys were arrested and several injured in the melee.

Their demonstration was followed by a more determined march by some 1,500 students of Korea University who clashed violently with police shortly after noon.

The students--and opposition political parties--have charged President Park's government with "selling out" to Japanese interests in the long negotiations to return normal diplomatic relations to the two nations.

President Park has declared that the treaty will be signed as planned in May.

The Koreans have long resented the Japanese because of the 45 years that Japan administered the affairs of Korea as a conquered nation.

The basic treaty worked out between the two nations calls for Japan to provide development loans and credit to Korea, and in return Korea would give up the arbitrary "free fishery line" that was drawn to keep Japanese fishing boats well away from Korean waters.

Student demonstrations were beginning to worsen even as the fifth anniversary celebration on April 19 of the student rebellion that overthrew President Syngman Rhee drew closer.

ART SALES RECORD SET

NEW YORK (UPI) - The world's auction records for a dozen top artists and "Sunday painters" including Sir Winston Churchill's were smashed last night at the most expensive art sale ever held.

The 26,000 dollars fetched by a landscape by the late British Statesman was dwarfed by prices like 410,000 dollars for a Degas, 224,000 dollars for a Van Gogh, and 155,000 dollars for a Bunnard, but the auction at the Parke-Bernet galleries proved that Sir Winston is an artist to be reckoned with in the rising art market.

A total of 2,855,000 dollars worth of paintings and sculpture changed hands last night at a double-header sale of 130 works with a formal 50-dollar a plate benefit dinner sandwiched between. More than 2,200 collectors and celebrities overflowed the galleries.

POLICE STOP SABOTAGE

SINGAPORE (UPI) - Police believe they foiled two Indonesian sabotage attempts Wednesday night, one of which nearly killed four bomb disposal men.

The demolition men ran for their lives when a 25 pound charge exploded as they were attempting to defuse another bomb.

A Defense Ministry spokesman in Kuala Lumpur said a total of five Indonesians were arrested.

Two of the men were arrested in Katong and three brothers were seized aboard a motorboat 300 yards from shore in the same region.

The spokesman said a second group, apparently making a sabotage bid, were caught by a customs launch.

Another Indonesian escaped a hail of bullets in the fast motorboat that brought the first sabotage group.

SPORTS

MAJOR LEAGUE STANDINGS

NATIONAL LEAGUE	W	L	AMERICAN LEAGUE	W	L
CHICAGO	2	0	DETROIT	2	0
PITTSBURGH	2	1	MINNESOTA	1	0
PHILADELPHIA	1	1	CLEVELAND	1	0
MILWAUKEE	1	1	WASHINGTON	1	1
CINCINNATI	1	1	BALTIMORE	1	1
HOUSTON	1	1	CHICAGO	1	1
SAN FRANCISCO	1	2	BOSTON	1	1
ST. LOUIS	0	2	NEW YORK	0	2
NEW YORK	0	2	KANSAS CITY	0	2

" WHY NOT? IT'S THE LATEST MIDWAY FAD!"

17 APR

Dear Mom + Dad,

I am fine and hope you are the same. I received your Easter card + gift yesterday. Thank you.

We have been busy here the last couple of days. We struck a dense jungle area in S. Vietnam, thought to be a Viet Cong stronghold. It is marked in the ship's daily newspaper. It seams that the East Coast doesn't get too much news about the Far East. And likewise we don't here a lot about Berlin either.

Yesterday we wiped out two bridges in N. Vietnam. Everyone got back safely.

Well I finally got my release orders. I will leave the squadron anytime after 12 MAY in order to be released by the 28th.

- I may try to stay at Jack & Carol's place for about a week to prepare my gear for shipment and also make a couple of trips to L.A. and SFran. about employment with the airlines. I'm pretty sure this is what I will try to do.

Then I will hop into my TR3 and make for home. I want to see everyone and also make our 5 yr. class reunion at B-W on 12 Jun.

- I hope those tornadoes didn't give you any trouble. From what I hear they really did a lot of damage.

Cubi Pt is in Subic Bay which is about 45 miles NW of Manila on the island of LUZON, The northern most isle in the Philippines.

Now we are operating near Da Nang in the Gulf of Tonkin.

- Rumor has it that our next port is Hong Kong. Sure would be good to get into there once again. It is a duty free port.

II. I hope Dad is feeling better.
   I probably will start sending some change of address cards to people. So you might start getting some of my mail.
   Well that is all for now.
                    Love,
                    Richard

24 APR

Dear Mom & Dad,

I am fine and hope you are the same. The weather out here is getting a little more humid, probably get worse.

Well last Easter Sun. I became a member of the Double Centurion club when I made my 200th landing aboard Midway. (Now have 204). The funny part about it was that it was at night. Oh well!

Operations are going at an even pace here. I fly a strike about every other day maybe two days. The C.O. is trying to keep the hops even between everybody. I hope we are doing some good. Everyone here and back in the U.S. (according to the Far East news) seem to have different ideas about it.

RICHARD CHERBA

II Thought you might want to keep the clipping so I am returning it.

Thank you for the card + gift again, I wish you wouldn't do it though because I don't need the money. I cann't spend it out here anyway.

Got a funny card from Barb. They went to Vegas for four days, I guess over spring vacation. Hope they have enough credit cards to get them back home.

Tell June + family I said hello. I know everyone reads these letters but there isn't enough material for separate letters all the time.

Well I'll close for now.

love,
Richard

4 MAY

Dear Mom + Dad,

I hope everyone at home is well. As for me I have been in bed all day with a touch of the flu or something. Really felt bad this morning, but after a few pills from Doc feel a little better now.

Received both of your letters today, don't bother to send the pics or clippings as I will be leaving the squadron on the 12th. We already have confirmed reservations to leave Clark AFB on the 14th and arrive at Travis AFB on the 14th in Calif. (Because of the date line)

April 30th I left the ship to go up to Atsugi, Japan to pick up an airplane for our squadron.

RICHARD CHERBA

I got back yesterday afternoon. It was kind of a long trip.

The reunion at B W is the year class of '60 graduates, not Fraternity. No I didn't know of Johnny Y. What was he trying to do?

The trip to the Fair sounds like a good idea, but I won't go by bus. I don't like to plan that for ahead.

Well I'll sign off for now, please excuse the writing.

Love,
Richard

HAPPY MOTHER'S DAY!

P.S. Hope you & Irene got the flowers.

7 MAY

Dear Mom + Dad,
Received your letter today so I thought I would answer it right away. I am feeling fine again, probably just a ~~long~~ touch of the Flu. Hope everyone at home is feeling better also.

The weather here has been so so. A little rain, a little sunshine

As for the airlines letters, which you may open, just hold them at home. I can fill them out if I want when I get home. I already have sent back 3 or 4. Keep them together so you can tell me about them over the phone when I call home.

As the schedule goes now we leave and arrive on the 14th of May. So I'll call as soon as I can and at a reasonable hour. Hank and I will probably go to Lemoore for the week end (pick up my car) and drive back to Alameda for processing on Monday.

Will close for now.

Love,
Richard

U·S·S· MIDWAY
CVA-41

18 MAY

Dear Mom + Dad,
  I am fine and hope everyone at home is too.
  I am a house guest of Jack & Carol right now.
  Yesterday I was in Alameda for separation processing. It only took 4 hours after we rushed them a bit. Seems it takes longer to get in then out. We left Alameda at 1215. I then took Hank to the S.F. airport where he flew back to Pensacola to meet Theresa².
  So now I am an unemployed civilian!
  I received a letter from TWA about an interview on 2 June.

So I am changing my plans slightly. I will be here at 30 Linda Ln. Lemoore until the Hancock comes in and I can get my bike. Then I will fly (at TWA's expense) to Kansas City for the interview. If I get hired I will work for them. Then I will fly back to Calif. and drive home.

I shipped 3 boxes home and they should arrive around the 11th of Jan. Bush Van Lines of Akron will be bringing them.

If I should happen to get my new Diners' Club card please forward it to me here. The one I have expires at the end of this month.

Well I paid $240⁰⁰ for the work I had done on my car. Cheaper than a new one. Besides I like to drive the TR.

Not too much else here. I might fly to Phoenix to see Fraz.

this week-end and then to Vegas for the Tailhook party. A big blast with all the Navy carrier pilots.

Bye for now,

Love,
Richard

RICHARD CHERBA

Holiday Inn of Spokane
4212 Sunset Boulevard
Spokane, Washington

6-15

Dear Mom & Dad,

Sorry to be so long in my writing. I am fine and hope you are the same. I have been on the go having a ball. — On Fri. Sat. & Sun. of Memorial day week-end. I flew (A-4) to Alameda and met a friend that I met at Bass a couple of years ago and we drove to Bass Lake. Stayed at the cabin. Howie Alexander and some other guys are renting it again this summer. He has his boat up there so naturally we did a lot of water skiing. The Pearson's were also up there so it was like old home week.

I had a few days off in the beginning of the month so I attended the 10th annual Tailhook

II Reunion at Las Vegas. There were about 800 carrier pilots in attendance. (Also went by A-4) Enjoyed being in the big city again. Saw the Lido 66 show at the Stardust hotel which is where the reunion was held. A lot of drinkin' + gamblin. Had a lot of fun.

In May I got 20 hrs. in the A-4 mostly on X-countries.

Last drill week end four of us launched out to Quonset Pt., Rhode Island to visit the Papa's. Hank was in Finland for a month with Pan American, but saw his wife and his folks. Stayed overnight at the Inn where Hank's Dad treated us to some beverages and a lobster dinner in his restaurant. Then came back to NSP Sun. A.M.

This Thursday I may have to fly to Pensacola to get refreshed in lo pressure chamber and ejection seat training.

I have a pretty good schedule this month. I go to work every Mon. at 1230 and get home on Thurs. at 5 p.m. with Fri. Sat + Sun. off. I have a total of 13 days off.

RICHARD CHERBA

III. I have a day layover in D.C. and Portland, with two short layovers in Detroit & Spokane. This last D.C. layover I had lunch with some people formerly in VA-22 that are now working in the Pentagon and Bureau of Weapons. CDR Smith — former C.O. —, ED Leighton and Chuck Jefferman.

On our Portland layover today we rented a V.W. and drove up to Mt. Hood recreation area just to see what the area was like around here. Really beautiful and cool. Some people were still snow skiing on some leftover snow.

Have you decided whether or not you will be going to Barb's wedding? I can get into McClellan AFB in Sac. with an A-4 and if I can

TV get the time off will get to the wedding.

Haven't had my boat out a lot. Really haven't been home. It is running good though.

Well that brings me up to date. Have to get up at 5:30 am so will go to bed now. Will try to write more often, but you know me.

Give my Love to all!

Love,
Richard

27 July

Dear Mom + Dad,

I am fine and hope everyone else is the same. Hope Brian is getting along with his cast.

I have been laid off since the 9th because of the strike. Don't quite know when it is going to end. I hope soon. The lay off came right in the middle of my co-pilot flight training. So it put me in a peculiar situation. I could have taken vacation, which I didn't want right now under these circumstances or be in a lay off status. So I chose the latter. As it turned out I was called back on the 21ST to fly a training trip and my final check ride on the 22ND. So now I am a fully qualified co-pilot but in layoff status again. The reason we were flying is because flight training is continuing to operate. It took me a little more than 8 hrs. to check out which is a little better than average I guess.

On the 15th I took a four day x country to Calif. + Wash.(state) Got back on the 19th. Stayed in San Fran for two days then Sun. night flew to Whidbey Island in Wash. to get a refresher in the low pressure chamber, Mon. aft. flew to Lemoore for an ejection seat refresher. Have to get

RICHARD CHERBA

II - these every two years. Stayed with Jack & Carol Oakes on Mon. night. Boy! is Nancy getting big. Hardly recognized her! Carol fixed some Tacos for dinner sure was good! Then Tues. I flew home. I got 5 extra dolls in which means the $ situation won't be too bad until after the middle of Aug. And my income tax return is due soon also.

I was going to drive home this week but a couple of charter flights came up. One yesterday to Duluth & back. And was supposed to go to Chicago today but weather was too bad. Probably will go to Chicago tomorrow. These trips pay $25-30 per day. So I can't afford to pass them up at this time.

The plane is a Cessna 206 single eng. prop. 6 passenger. It belongs to a broker in Minneapolis.

Four of us are checked out in it and will fly it whenever he needs us. He probably be able to get a hold of one of us if the other three are working. We all work for N.W. In fact the Tues. after the strike the four of us took the airplane up to Ashland Wis. which is on Lake Superior. Played some golf in the A.M. Then in the afternoon, we got the owner's boat, a 26' Chris Craft cruiser on the lake for some swimming and cruising. We came home about 10 pm. We had a great day!

The first seven days in Aug. I have a chance to go on active duty for some special flying to evaluate the lo level flying that the Navy etc. does. The tests will be in Louisianna. So I will get full pay + expenses for this, too. And I also have some extra drills left so I can get them in next

II. month also. I also have started the processing to drive a Yellow Cab. But haven't had the chance to finish yet. Could make $10-15 a day, not much but it will be enough. Probably won't get started on this until next month.

And in my free time, the boat has been in the water, and we have been doing a lot of water skiing. Have a decent tan for a change. And drinking a lot of beer. I bought a new competition ski and it is really great to ski on.

My roomies and I thank you for the CARE package. It was well received and arrived on the 22nd. The letter took about 3 days.

In Calif. I talked with Jim B's Dad, he said that Barb & Jim caught a flight home the night before the strike. B & I had driven to Sac. so I didn't get to see them.

    When I talked to Dad last he mentioned the Honda, then I thought about it and he cannot get the license without the 65 registration so it is enclosed.

    Also stamps from Madagascar. My roommate has a brother there.

    I think I'm caught up now so I'll close until next time.
    Give my love to all,
            Love,
            Richard

5 AUG

Dear Mom + Dad,
    Just a few lines to say hello and I am fine.
    I got the forwarded mail today.
    Kind of warm up here now. Went water skiing last Sunday with a former Navy pilot + his wife. They had dinner too. Spagetti. They bought a $30,000 house and pay $75.00 a mo. just for property TAX. Minn. doesn't have any sales tax. Really high, isn't it?
    School this week isn't bad as we are going over a few things I already knew.
    Not too much else to report. Sorry the letter is so short.

                Love,
                Richard

16 AUG 65

Dear Mom + Dad,

I am fine and hope you are the same. It has been pretty warm up here. Even went skiing yesterday on one of the 10,000 lakes of Minn. Water was warm. Even have been using the pool here at the apts. for some refreshing relief.

I did get a copy of the Life mag. Paul and the Skipper really looked good.

That bulb sure lasted a few years in the proj. Too bad they always go when you need them.

I heard the other day that they store boats for the winter in a locked bldg. at the fair grounds in St. Paul. Cost only $15-20. Have to be in there in Oct. and out by April. I'll have to check into it.

II.
I do appreciate you forwarding my mail. I got the 1st pkg. I had to pick it up at the P.O. 5¢ post. due. The second one is also there with 15¢ post. due. Now I really don't mind paying the postage, but I really have to drive to get there before it closes at 5 pm. I don't get out of work until 4:30 or so, so please check the postage. Thank you. I have also been getting the regular mail that has been forwarded.

Enclosed is a copy of the bill for the tape recorder. It has been paid by me and Commercial Frt also is getting a copy and I have the original. They should foot the entire bill.

If they call find out what you can but also have them write me.

Well school hasn't been bad too far. It is kind of spoonfed and the tests are right from the lectures. In fact some times he even tells you

III

It is a test question. Sometimes it gives me a false sense of security but some of the material is brand new to me and still requires a bit of effort.

The first week was studying company ground and flight procedures and rules and regulations.

Last week we began to learn all the various systems of the Lockheed Electra, 4 eng. turbo-prop (HALF JET HALF PROP). It was supposed to be a 2 week school but tomorrow afternoon we start the Boeing 727 school (3 jet engines) and finish the Electra some other time. Nobody can tell us why. So we just go on.

Class start at 8:45am to 4:30pm 6 (5½) days a week. Man, those week ends are really short. I've got calluses on my ___ ___!

They have a good cafeteria for lunch. Dinners are usually

30 AUG 65

Dear Mom + Dad,
I am fine and hope you are the same. The flight home was uneventful. It is a little diff. in the cockpit then back in the passenger cabin.

The weather here sure has been lousy. Rain, cold, drizzle. I believe the state is going to skip Fall and go from summer to Winter. BRRR!!!

Saw where the strike is going to be delayed 8 days. Hope it gets settled.

Yes I did get a call from Jack + Carol the other night they will be up here between the 20 & 27 of Sept. They will be able to spend two days. They want me to pick the two days, I don't believe they will be going to Ohio. But you never know. I am going to let them know around the 10th.

I don't know what to do about the gear in Calif. I think I'll just have it sent here because I don't know when I would be able to get home with a car to bring that stuff up here.

That's it for now, tell Irene, Gordon & Brian I said hello.

Love,
Richard

P.S. Had to open letter again. I am cancelling the ins. on the Honda. Kind of stupid to have it now. It wasn't ins. for fire or theft anyhow.

RICHARD CHERBA

60¢ a 85¢ or you can go thru the sandwich line. So lunch costs me from 60¢ to $1.00 (about) a day. Pretty reasonable.

At home here we have been doing some cooking. Last night the neighbor gal (about 250 lbs), put a roast on the charcoal rotisserie. So six of us had a beef dinner. Really good.

Well, that's up to date. Please understand about the mail.

I'll sign off for now. Oh yes. Let <u>me</u> worry about Reverend.

Love,
Richard

P.S. My love to the Sooy's also!

P.S.

Got the windshield for my boat. Costs only $50.

A couple of fellows help me put it on one night, also put on the top. Really looks sharp!

Bye

Love
Richard

7 Sep.

Dear Mom + Dad,
    I am fine and hope everyone at home is the same. Started to write TUES. but kept putting it off. So before I go to work this A.M. I'll dash off a few lines.

    I have a pretty good schedule this mo. I should draw #1 (senior) second officer on the B727. It won't be that way long though because hopefully next mo. I will be able to bid a Co-pilot schedule. I will have 17 days off this mo. and fly to Newark and return. Do this 3 days in a row then

II have 4 days off. Tuff huh!!

Had a real nice holiday weekend. Put the boat in the Miss. River and went all the way to Winona, Minn. and back. 236 miles, round trip. Left on Sat. 3 pm and got home on Mon. evening about 7:30. Slept on the boat, saw a lot of the river, went through 5 locks. All in all it was an adventurous journey and really enjoyed it.

The weather here is in the mid 70's so it looks like fall will soon be here although will try to ski one more once.

Had my first call the other AM to sub teach but had

III to fly. So I didn't make it.
Just finished a late breakfast.
I have my eye on another house on the lake. One bedroom house with a fireplace 100 ft lakeshore by 145' 250' deep.

They are asking $14,9 but I may be able to get it for 13. or 14. Don't know if I want it yet though. The lakeshore is really nice. I can probably get it with $1000 dn. which I already have. Payments of $145.00 a month. Will be looking into it further and keep you posted.

Well I will close for now. I hope Johnny G holds

off on the marriage. He doesn't bring home a lot of money. Oh well, bye for now.

        Love,
        Richard

RICHARD CHERBA

12 SEP.

Dear Mom & Dad,

I am fine and hope you are the same.

The weather is lousy, it rained all day today. Our class got together and had a beer bust on the St. Croix River in Wisconsin. (only an hour from here). The gals fixed some hot dogs & salad and of course the keg of beer. It was at a farm house on the river so we had someplace to go when the drops began. Fireplace, too.

I got the package of mail, also the bonds & money. Thank

II you. Although all I needed was the bonds.

If possible do you think you could send the guns to me parcel post. If you do, insure it for whatever it was insured for before. There are two guns in the package. a shotgun and a rifle.

This week is the big push for the written sometime Fri. or Mon.

Fray is getting married in Kansas City on 25 SEP. Sure would like to be there for that one. But I think (hope) to be in Miami for 10 days of flight training.

Close for now. Thank you again.

Love,
Richard

Sun.

Dear Mom & Dad,
 I am fine and hope you are the same.
 The weather here is rather chilly. The temps have been in the 50-70° range. More in the lower.
 Sat. we finished B727 school. So now we have about a week of study for the Flight Engineer written exam.
 Guess what I found in my black sweater? The garage key. I'll return it on my next trip home.
 Happened to be at the airport one day (Fri) when one of the gds gents was buying a ticket. So who should happen to come thru the door but Dan Geldner. He just

I got out of the Navy. He also was in VA-22 and just returned from V.Nam.

I don't know if you've heard yet but Skip Brumbaver my former roommate in Lemoore and in VA-22 was shot down. I don't know if he is OK or what. They are not sure if they saw a chute. I sure don't feel too good about leaving the squadron early like I did. I'd sure like to be giving them hell for all the close friends that have been missing or killed in action, or POWs.

Well I'm going to need some extra money to catch up on my ins. + gas bills from my trip from Calif. So if you would please forward my last two (2) bonds that were issued ($50⁰⁰ types) I would appreciate it. Thank you.

III I'll close for now. I did get the mail, Playboy etc. Say hello to Irene & family for me.
    Love,
    Richard

Miami Beach. 9/26/65. Hi, Getting some sun and taking a dip in the pool every day. Haven't been to the beach yet but would like to try it one night. Training is coming along. Still haven't found out if we passed the test yet. Love Richard.

North Beach. 10/14/65. Back again to finish up. Came down last Friday. Raining right now, so we are not at the pool. Guess MPS is getting colder. Love, Richard

RICHARD CHERBA

10-3-65

Dear Mom + Dad,
    I am fine and hope you are the same.
    This last week 4 of us moved into a house – 3 bedroom – furnished. It really is nice, has a lot of room, radiant heating, no basement.
    New address is
        7638 NICOLLET AVE.
        MINNEAPOLIS 23, MINN
            55423

Phone is same 866-3554
    code - 612

We built a huge bookcase at one end of the living room. 8' long and 38" high. Looks good.
    Would like to get home soon

and try to pick up the stereo, drums + desk. But as yet don't know when.

As far as the exam went I dropped one part out of 5. So I had to come back to MSP to retake it. But I passed the second time so now I am ready to complete my flight training. May have to return to Miami. Tough break!!!

I did see Schaughs, they drove down Sat. night. and then on Sun. I took an airport limosine to Ft. Laud. to spend the day with them. She sure was glad to see me. Georgie is really a whiz! Went swimming together and played with him. He got a kick out of it.

Well the weather here has finally cleared up. We have had 3

RICHARD CHERBA

3 straight days of sunshine. Even washed the car and mowed the grass. The sun felt good and warm.

I feel kind of bad not sending Irene's a birthday card or anniv. card. But we took the exam on the 17th. And I studied more for that than I did for anything at B-W.

Hope Dad is feeling better. Glad he decided to see the Doctor.

Who painted the kitchen?

The post cards are one of the main hotel and the plane I will be working on.

Will close for now. Oh yes also took communion today at the Methodist church. Bye

Love,
Richard

1 NOV

Dear Mom & Dad,

I am fine and hope everyone at home is too.

We got home about 1pm Sat. night. We had excellent seats on the 30 yard line and saw all but the last 3 min. of the game. We (the crew) had to beat the crowd out of the stadium and get to the airport. The Gophers lost and so did the Browns we watched the game on TV Sunday.

You'll notice the letter is being written in ink but still in the familiar chicken scratch. Today I received a beautiful Shaeffer desk pen set with a cartridge pen. It is from VA-22 and I guess is part of my going away gift. It has a brass inscription:

LT. DICK CHERBA
A FIGHTING REDCOCK DEC 62 - MAY 65
FROM THE OFFICERS OF VA-22

I. It will be a nice momento from the squadron.

I got most of my gear put away and it all got here in good condition.

The house is just great we have 3 couches and lots more furniture.

I have a fairly good schedule for Nov. I spend a total of 8 or so days in Detroit throughout the mo.

We leave here at 5:05 go to Det. then Newark, N.J. then back to Det. where we spend 21 hrs on a layover leave the next night for MSP with a stop at Milwaukee first. We do this several times in this mo. I have a total of about 13 days off.

The best part of the schedule is near the end of the mo. when I have a 22 hr. layover in Cleveland. So I'll be home on Thanksgiving. I'll arrive on FLIGHT 560 WED the 24th at 1103 P.M. and will leave the following night at 855 P.M.

Well, not to much else to report except who do I know around Det. that I could visit.

When you come down on the 24th I'll be able to show you the airplane. The next day I won't have any time.

Well bye for now, hope you weren't rushed by all the Halloweeners.

Love,
Richard

RICHARD CHERBA

7 NOV.

Dear Mom + Dad,
　I am fine and hope you are the same.
　I'm glad you enjoyed the trip up here and please never worry about the little things. I love you the way you are and wouldn't want it any other way. You know I never pay attention to the way other people think or act. I have too many big things to worry about.
　That's the trouble with some people and why they get ulcers. etc. Worry too much. I take and live life as it comes good or bad.

II. And I probably always will. Anyway I and everyone you met enjoyed your company only sorry you couldn't have come earlier or stayed longer.

Not too much to worry about as far as the ride to Chicago. We are ready for those things, but you really should use the masks when they come down. Your useful conscious time is only 10-15 min. at the altitudes we fly at. Normally the cabin is kept at 5-6000 ft. above 14 thousand the masks drop down. This is why your ears popped. You ~~suppress~~ experience a small decompression. This is my guess. I tried to find out about the flight but didn't

III get any answers.

Got a letter from Rodger Simonian. He got married to a gal in San. Fran. Now doing 6 mos. in the Army at Olympia Wash.

Getting ready to close the deal on the lots. Having an attorney check over the title etc.

This last drill week-end we (4) went to San Diego got back yesterday p.m. (sun)

This month I have short layovers in DC + Detroit. We also fly to Winnipeg Canada.

Well bye for now, will write again soon.

        Love,
        Richard

20 Nov

Dear Mom + Dad,

I am fine and hope you are the same. The weather here was rather nice today. Although everyone here is sort of looking forward to some snow and some winter skiing. We went to a ski show at the auditorium on Fri. night. Looked at some boots and ski equip.

I don't know where I will be on Thanksgiving. Probably in Detroit. Have a nice day anyway. Wish I could be home. I received a nice card from Aunt Marge + Uncle Fred.

Well I sent the balance of the down payment for the lot. So

It looks like I am a property owner. ~~to~~ (without house). But that will come next summer.

I sure was nice for Jack & Ead to sent the nuts. Also got the notice on my insurance.

Not too much else for now. Will sign off.

Love,
Richard

10 Dec

Dear Mom and Dad,
    Hope everyone is well at home. I am feeling fine, too. Thought I would practice up on my typing-- I need it!

    Thought xx you might be interested in my schedule for Dec. It's No.113. As you can see I got home Tue. night (about 10 pm) and don't have to work again until Mon. Aft. Pretty tuff week. I was thinking of coming home but I wasn't sure whether the car would make it and payday isn't until Mon. One other reason was I wanted to get some flight time at NAS Twin Cities. I don't know if I told you or not but I am a Weekend Warrior in the Naval Reserve. the squadron is VA-811. They fly the A4B which is the same type I flew while I was on active duty. Well the weather here has been pretty bad in that it has been cloudy and some fog. The temp. has been around 35°.

    The flying will boost my income a little because we get full pay for the weekends plus we get paid when we fly at any other time. For instance, for spending three hours on the station we get about $23.00, 8 hours, double or 46.00. The only trouble with it is that they only pay quarterly. But as soon as I get 20 hours in the A4 to build up my proffiecency (?) I will be able to take cross countries anywhere I like. I would like to run out to Lemoore to see the squadron VA-22 and welcome them back.

    Well the mailman just came and brought me my Air medal and citation. Whee! Dan Gildner got 10 of them but he also flew 99 combat missions. I'll bring it home so that you can see it. Think I'll hang it in the bathroom!

    Speaking of getting home, I will be home the weekend before Christmas also. I will get into Cle on Flight 560 from Chicago at 1103 pm Fri the 17th. Leave on Sun. at 1130.

RICHARD CHERBA

II

On the 24th I arrive on Flt 500 from Chicago at 1053 am. Leave Sun. at 1130 am. Of course you realize that all this is subject to change at the companies' needs so don't be disappointed if the schedule changes. I believe I will be spending New Year's Eve in Seattle Wash.

I think I saw the same picture on the A4.

Cann't think of anything else right now. So I'll close, the typing and spelling really need some work. See you Friday. will call if anything changes.

Oh yes, read about those fireballs around there in this am's paper. Did you see any?

love
Richard

30 DEC.

Dear Mom & Dad,
 I am fine and hope everyone at home is too. Sorry about Christmas but it is just one of those things that you can't foresee.

 Enclosed you will see my Jan. schedule. It is a series of 12 hr. layovers in Cle also two 36 hr. layovers in Cle on the 8th and 22nd. They are all FLT. 560 from Chicago and arrive at 11:03 p.m. in Cle. On the 12 hr. layovers I have to be at the airport by 10:30 AM the following day to get FLT. 500. Not too many days off but the working hrs are good except for one flight where I have to get up at 2 AM AUUUGH!

 So depending on weather etc. and if you want to make some trips to the airport I should see you a lot. Would like to see you on the 3rd so I can see your Xmas present.

I —

Got a card from Dave and she told me about her plans. Says she is also at a new address.

The weather here has been quite nice. Upper 40's, lower 50's although it has been foggy. No snow!

By the way I've picked up the $60's for you on my check.

That's about it for now. See you on the 30th. I arrive here in Seattle. Leave tonight midnight in Oakland then to Seattle the next day and then head back home on the 1st.

Love,
Richard

This was my Christmas card to my parents in 1965, the first year on NWA as a second officer on the engineer panel. 3rd seat on the Boeing-727. I might also have done this on a layover in CLE. Just a piece of cardboard from the back of a tablet.

LETTERS

**From Richard Cherba
to My Parents John & Irene Cherba
From MSP**

1966

1965?

23 FEB. 66

Dear Mom + Dad,
    I am fine and hope that Dad is getting better.
    It is a warm 27° outside, pretty warm, huh! The temps haven't been bad the last week or so, and I believe that my blood must be getting used to it.
    Haven't been doing much as of late. Work is going well, if you can call it work. Also have been doing some flying out at NAS.
    I go to work this p.m., leave at 4:45 to Chicago, Cle, then Phil. Stay overnite then go to Det. - Phil, Cle, Chicago and get home about 9 am. I have the same trip all this month.
    I have from Fri. until Tues. pm. off so I am taking an A-4 to Alameda for two days. Leave Fri. AM and come back Sun. night.

II

Thought I would hit the city of bright lights for a couple of days San Fran.

I don't know what my schedule will be for next month yet.

Well I can't think of anything else right now so I'll close for now.

        Love,
        Richard

3 MAR 66

Dear Mom + Dad,
I am fine and hope you are the same. Is Dad still sitting with his leg propped up? Well I got back from 3 days in San Fran. last Sun. night. Stayed with Rodger. We hit the Playboy Club and other joints in the big city. Sat. I flew down to Lemoore and visited with the CO. VA-22, OAKES and the Pearsons. Also ran into Paul Ilg at Nas Alameda. So I had a good time.
March finds me flying West. I have Portland and Chicago layovers. I only drive to work 6 times and have 14 days off. Not bad.
I don't know when I will be home next.

The weather here has been warm 35-45° ABOVE. It is raining now, probably will turn into snow.

Glad to hear your paintings were well received. When will you start with its?

Hope your rug is in now.

Well that is about it for now. Will write again soon.

Love,
Richard

RICHARD CHERBA

HAPPY APRIL FOOL'S   1 APR
        1967   DAY
              3 pm.
Dear Mom + Dad
        I am fine and hope you are the same. It sure is trying to warm up here, the wind is really blowing though.
        Well in the month of April I drive to work seven times and gone from noon until 6:30pm two days later about 54 total hrs. Each trip has a 14 hr Portland layover and a 17 hr. Cle. layover. 13 days off, about 2 off between each trip.
        I will normally come in on #560 - 11:03pm on the 6, 11, 21. Right now I plan to drive home on the 17th but have to be back on the 20th. I'll have to look at it closer when the time comes so don't really plan on it too much. As for Palm + Easter I have to work.
        Oh yes, we may stay downtown on the Cle. layovers. Don't know for sure.

II

Sort of anxious to get the boat out and get it in shape. Went to the Boat show here in Mpls. yesterday. Not as good as the ones in Chi. that I remember. There is sure a lot to do here in the summer. They have 2-3 day canoe trips on the Canadian Border. $7⁰⁰ a day includes everything except clothes + tackle. Sounds good!!

Glad to hear that Dad is feeling better. You should take it easy for a while.

Sounds like you are starting your own art school.

I drill this week-end.

Not too much else right now. Hope to see you on the 6th or 7th.

Love,
Richard

MAY DAY!

1 MAY

Dear Mom & Dad,
    I am fine and hope you all are too.

    Got back from a cross country this afternoon. Two of us left for Pensacola, Fri. When I got down there I ran into Hank Papa and his wife and spent the night at her folks beach house on Perdido Bay. Fresh shrimp and oysters, water skiing and swimming. Really had a great time! Then we were on our way to San Diego and had to stop at Beeville, Texas (Chase) for gas only to find our starting probe went bad. So we spent the night there and left this A.M. for Minneapolis. But at Chase ran into Dave & Kay Hill formerly of VA-22. So it turned out to be an enjoyable week-end.

The picture was taken here at Twin Cities. Sorry about the fold.

About a week ago, we all went to see & hear the Tyuana Brass. We have all of their records. It was a good concert.

My next 3 weeks will be spent in ground school for the Boeing 720-320. I don't know if I will get qualified in it or not.

Still looking for a house, but no luck. I don't know what you should do. If you want to move sell, if not stay there. I don't know which way you would get the best deal.

Not much else, oh yes. Jack & Carol Oakes will be up between May 10-14 to spend a few days. They are taking two weeks vacation and touring the Western states.

Will sign off for now.

Love,
Richard

June 5, 1966

OCT. 18

Dear Mom + Dad,
I am fine and hope you are the same.
I got home from Miami Fri. night.
Last Tues. I had my oral exam and then on Thurs. my flight check, both given by the FAA. So now I have my Flight Engineer's Certificate. On Fri. A.M. I got 30 min. of Co-pilot time and even got to land the B727. Really a nice airplane. This was also a part of the training. On the flight home and on Sat. I got the rest of my safety time by the company, so now I'm ready to fly regular line trips.
For the rest of this month I will probably be on call for trips. But next month should be able to hold

a schedule. I am off until Tues. noon but then will have to remain on call.

I think I will like it. You really work while flying but you also get a lot of time off.

I didn't call Aunt Julia while I was in the South. I didn't have time to go see them anyway. I will have to write a letter.

Glad to hear that Dad is feeling fine again. First chance I can get I will be home. Probably not until next month.

I'm waiting for my gear from Calif. It is supposed to be here this P.M.

Well keep your thumb out of doors, I mean be careful.

P.S. TEMP. IS **76°** Really beautiful.

Bye for now.
Love,
Richard

28 Nov.

Dear Mom + Dad,

Well I got home yesterday about 4 p.m. There was a little snow on the ground and the temp. was a cool +15°. BRRR!!!

I enjoyed being home and want to thank you for everything including the roll I took with me. Everybody here liked it.

Well, some other good news, I bid for a Dec. schedule and got Det. layovers again but at Xmas I have a long layover in Cle. so will see you again. I misplaced the schedule so will have to let you know more about it later.

Nothing else for right now so will sign off.

Love,
Richard

30 DEC.

Dear Mom & Dad,
 I am fine and hope everyone at home is too. Sorry about Christmas but it is just one of those things that you cann't foresee.

 Enclosed you will see my Jan. schedule. It is a series of 12 hr. layovers in Cle. also two 36 hr. layovers in Cle. on the 8th and 22nd. They are all FLT. 560 from Chicago and arrive at 11:03 p.m in Cle. On the 12 hr. layovers I have to be at the airport by 10:30 AM the following day to get FLT. 500. Not to many days off but the working hrs are good all except for one flight where I have to get up at 2 AM AUUUGH!

 So depending on weather, etc. and if you want to make some trips to the airport I should see you a lot. I would like to see you on the 3RD so I can give you your xmas present.

II

Got a card from Barb. and she told me about her plans. Says she is also at a new address.

The weather here has been quite warm upper 30's & lower 40's although it has been foggy. No snow!

By the way I've ticked all the 560's for you on my schedule.

That's about it for now, see you on the 3RD. Spend N.Y. eve in Seattle. Leave tonight, overnight in Portland then to Seattle the next day. and then head back home on the 1.ST

Love,
Richard

LETTERS

**From Richard Cherba
to My Parents John & Irene Cherba
From MSP**

1967

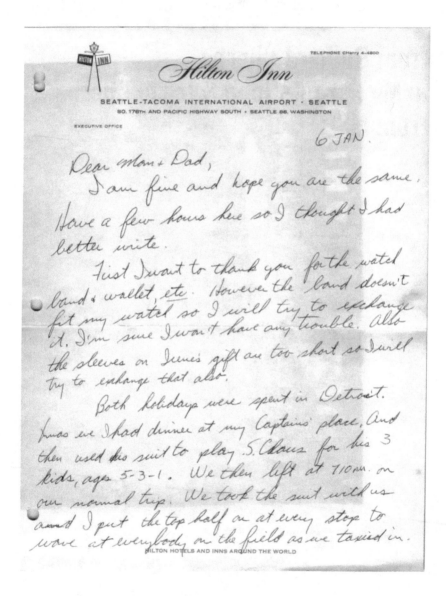

6 JAN.

Dear Mom & Dad,

I am fine and hope you are the same. Have a few hours here so I thought I had better write.

First I want to thank you for the watch band & wallet, etc. However the band doesn't fit my watch so I will try to exchange it. I'm sure I won't have any trouble. Also the sleeves on Irene's gift are too short so I will try to exchange that also.

Both holidays were spent in Detroit. Xmas eve I had dinner at my Captain's place. And then used his suit to play S. Claus for his 3 kids, ages 5-3-1. We then left at 7:10 AM. on our normal trip. We took the suit with us and I put the top half on at every stop to wave at everybody on the field as we taxied in.

I would stick my head out the window. We sure had lots of fun.

I have been snow-skiing twice already. I bought my own ski equipment so I am all set up. It sure is a lot of fun. Also got a few hours in Miami on Mon. Even got a little sunburn. I picked the trip up because I was a little short on time. This month I will be flying West to Portland and Seattle.

Well we should be all set to move by the end of the month. Bob & Jeff will be moving with me. Their rent will just about take care of my house payments until they decide to move. I'm sorry I don't have the pictures but I must have misplaced them. As soon as I can I'll get them to you.

The new address will be:
1340 VINE PLACE
MOUND, MINN.

Don't know the zip code yet. The drive to work will be about 35-40 min. But most of it is 4 lane. Along the same highway that I took you on when you

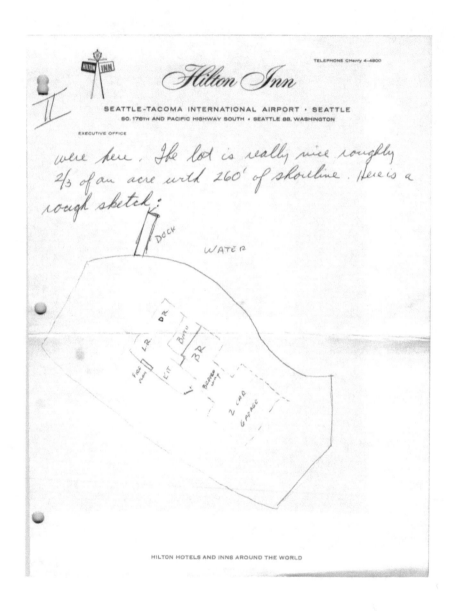

My neighbors have a couple of horses so we may also be doing a little riding.

Also in Feb. (13-26) I will be going to Fallon, Nev. for our annual two week cruise with the Naval reserve. I have been down to Kansas City to see Bob Frazier and his wife a couple of times and he is doing well. Works for TWA.

Well I will close for now.

Love,
Richard

1-18

Dear Mom + Dad,

Just a short note to say hello and that I am fine. Although just a bit chilly. The temp. got down to MINUS 31 last night. and tonight the same story. Naturally my car (not Bob's - he didn't go to work) didn't start either. I got home from work about 5 pm. - car started ok then. I don't have to go out until Fri noon. So I really didn't need it. We both tried to get them going all day but finally gave up. Drank beer instead.

Flying out West this month. We have a day layover in Portland, Oregon, so the last time we went up to the Mt. Hood Recreation Area about 60 miles East of Portland and did some snow skiing.

III. I had a real nice frame made for your watercolor, glasproof glass and all. The P.O. will be paying for most of it. The picture really looks good and everyone that sees it says it is good. I'm rather proud to say that you painted it.

I had the watchband fixed to fit my watch. Looks good. Thanks again. Please don't do anything for my birthday! Irene's either.

Glad to hear that Dad is feeling better. I hope he just takes it easy.

The sale of the house looks very promising. I don't envy a move after what I know I have to go thru. Especially since you have to move everything.

I did not call the Schlaugh's because we really weren't scheduled to be there that long and we got in at 2 AM in the AM.

IV We also are playing some cards tonight. Just a friendly little game.

Well I will close out for now before I break a record.

Love,
Richard

26 FEB

Dear Mom & Dad,
I am fine, just a little chilly, after spending the last two weeks in a fairly mild climate, like no snow and no temps below 0°F.

The two weeks went well. We got a lot of work done and all the pilots qualified in everything we attempted also got a 40.5 hrs average per pilot which is the highest any squadron has ever got.

We played, too. Spent both weekends in L. Vegas. Saw Phyllis Diller, Kim Sisters and some real good lounge shows.

I hope everyone is well at home. Last Thursday I flew to Moffett just South of Frisco and called Barb & Jim so Jim picked "up

II and visited with them for a couple of hours. The next morning we stopped at Lemoore before heading for L.V.

This next month I have D.C. layovers. I wasn't around to bid so I had my roommate bid for me.

That is about it for now. My love to everyone.

Love,
Richard

RICHARD CHERBA

18 MAR

Dear Mom + Dad,

I am fine and hope everything and everyone at home is fine, too.

Still a little cold up here but haven't had any more snow. (Hope!) Everything is going along fine. I put in a garbage disposal yesterday. It wasn't much of a job but it took a while. I got it at cost so it was a pretty good deal. $34.00

The drive to work takes about 40 min. (35 miles). It isn't bad and the scenery is quite nice.

I will try to get home soon. But not sure when. Maybe for Easter but don't really get the hopes up. I have to switch a day of ground school to give me about 4 days off. It may take an act of Congress. We will see.

Returning the 'art' announcement,

I cannot remember whether you wanted it or not. Also pictures of me at Xmas time as S. Claus. You can keep the color (one of Irene) but I would like the B+W whenever you get finished with them - No Hurry!

The color was taken at Sharon's home on Xmas eve. The rest on my trip.

That's it for now. Will close out.

Love,
Richard

7-25

Dear Mom + Dad,
I am fine and hope you are the same. I have tried to call a couple of times from Cle. but either busy or no answer.
Pam is up here now and has rented a room near the airport. Her Mother is also coming up here the first of Aug. and both of them will stay here at home. She is also supposed to drop you a line with the info you wanted (dress color- etc.)
We also need the following addresses. 1. Freddy Bingelli
2. Allen Boris
3. Peter Dancisko
4. Harry Novak
5. Goodsites
6. Chelucks

7. Al Harman
8. Nielsen (Gable)

The Sample is of the Brides'maid' dresses.

Pam says hello

Invitations will be sent to all people on the list you gave Pam except the - NAGY Boys
Ignatz's

If you want the list back. Let me know.

Bye for now,
Love
Richard

4 Aug. 1967

Dear Mom + Dad,
We are fine, hope everyone is OK at home. What about Irene?
As for the cake, Pam wants it all white.
Fray is bringing his wife Barb. So we will need 3 rooms for sure at the Motel. All for one night only.
Pam + I think we should have the extra 25 reserv. just in case. We will pay for it. As for as the time people can just stand around and chat. We will have to take pics anyway.
Are you supposed to get an invite? We have some if you would like one for keeping.

Pam thinks your pink dress sounds pretty.

Rehearsal dinner I count 13.
Bridal Party   6
Parents   4
Dean Gordon   2
Bob's wife   1
                —
                13

Pam picked up the dress yesterday. All invites should be out. Hope we didn't forget anybody.

Pam's Mother says Hi!
Pam says Hi!
I say good-bye for now
Love
Richard +
PAM

My swearing in to the Navy, at Naval Air Station Gross Isle MI. Navy paid my way from Cleveland to Detroit, then Gross Isle so that I could take a battery of tests, including a physical. After I completed the tests, the Navy said that I was qualified. And did I want to join up right then. I explained that I only had very little school left and both I and my parents were looking forward to the graduation ceremony. Told me I could sign up and arrangements made for that to happen. So here I am taking the oath. June 18, 1960.

I had always wanted to join the Navy and "See the World" and got to do this by joining the Navy and becoming a Naval Aviator.

Upon our arrival at Naval School of Pre-Flight in Pensacola, we began 16 weeks of ground school to learn the Navy customs, traditions, etiquette.

During the 16 weeks of Pre-Flight, there is a load of training. We were in Pensacola and there were hangars on the beach, concrete ramps into the water to accommodate the float planes that were able to taxi up the ramp into the hangar. We would do a lot of running there as well as hanging on pipe for as long as the drill instructor required. There was a step test, vertical jumping, and the 'o' course. Obstacle course. This was run in the sand and you had to complete it in the prescribed time. If not, we could practice it during our free time in the evening.

Cadet Cherba, cadet barracks. Only Line Officer has star on shoulder board.

There were two different distinctions in the cadet classes. If you were a college graduate you were an AOC. Aviation Officer Candidate. If you were only a 2 year college student you were a Cadet.

Upon completing Pre-Flight an AOC received his Ensign Gold Bar and commission. You also received about $400/mo. for pay. As a Cadet you were classified as an enlisted man and received the same pay as a white hat would. They would get their commission, gold bar and become an Officer. When they got their Wings of Gold. Of course their pay would also go up. Says some thing about getting a college 4 year degree. We were assigned to Saufley Airfield FL to begin pilot training in the T-34 Mentor aircraft. Some classes first about the airplane and my first hop was on November 8, 1960. Your first solo flight is scheduled for hop number 13. For me that was on December 16, 1960. There were a total of 33 flights. My last T-34 flight was on January 20, 1961.

There was a tradition that when you got your commission and gold Ensign bar that you gave your drill sergeant a silver dollar. He gave us our first salute which we returned. Enlisted sailors are to give the salute first to officers then returned. A very nice tradition.

I was now assigned to a different airfield to begin flight training in a T-28 at Whiting Field FL in Milton FL. February 2, 1961, Mom and Dad' 25th anniversary. And my 23rd birthday. My first flight in the T-28 was on February 1, 1961. I had 81 total training flights. 14 of those were carrier training and qualification flights. I got my first carrier landing in the T-28, June 16,1961. We had 8 carrier landings on the USS Antietam CV-36. and deck launched (no cat shot) 8 times. No catapult. Did a lot of practice on a field runway with a mirror aid. Mirror is pictured later.

The next was Chase Field in Beeville TX. My first flight in the F-9F8T was July 17, 1961 at Chase Field, in Beeville TX. Here I got 95 training flights. Also my first 6 carrier landings aboard the

USS Antietam on October 3,1961. Which was cruising in the Gulf of Mexico. Here the launch was a steam catapult. My last F-9 flight Nov.1,1961

We stayed at Chase to transition to our last training aircraft the F11, 23 training hops and 25 hours. At Chase Field.This was a supersonic fighter. We practiced air/air gunnery on a banner that was towed by another aircraft. We did go supersonic.

NAS Pensacola FL. Received Ensign commission after successful completion of vigorous 16 week course of instruction at Naval School of Pre-Flight at Pensacola FL. 10/28/60

NAAS Saufley Field FL 10/28/60

WINGS OF LEGACY

USS Antietam CV-36

Service Personnel

James H. Newell, son of Mr. and Mrs. James M. Newell, 425 Woodland Ave., recently was promoted to acting sergeant in Germany where he is a member of the 261st Engineer Co. Newell, a mess steward in the company in Furth, entered the Army in 1957 and was last stationed at Ft. Belvoir, Va. He went overseas in July, 1958. His wife, Martha, is with him in Germany.

Ensign Richard J. Cherba, USNR, received his commission upon successful completion of a 16-week course of instruction at the Naval School of Pre-flight at NAS Pensacola, Fla., and is now working on dual flights. He was graduated with a BME degree from Baldwin-Wallace College in June. His parents are Mr. and Mrs. John Cherba, 2223 North Ridge Rd., Elyria 7. His service address is Ens. Richard J. Cherba, USNR, B. O. Qu 838, Room 309, NAAS, Saufley Field, Pensacola, Fla.

Service Personnel

Pvt. Michael D. Gula has completed his basic training at Ft. Knox, Ky., and will continue his training there. He is the son of Mr. and Mrs. Michael G. Gula, 519 Bond St. His new address is: Pvt. M. D. Gula, US 52510508, Box 10, Co. E, 2nd Bn. School Regt. USAARMS Tm 4, Ft. Knox, Ky.

Staff Sergeant Leo R. Radley, son of Mrs. Agnes L. Thatcher, Ridgeway, is a member of the 2d Armored Calvary Regiment in Germany. He is assigned to Troop I of the regiment's 3d Reconnaissance Squadron in Amberg, arriving overseas on this tour of duty in September 1958. Sergeant Radley, who entered the Army in 1946, is a graduate of Wellington High School.

Navy Ens. Richard J. Cherba, son of Mr. and Mrs. John Cherba of 2223 North Ridge Rd., Elyria made his first solo flight last month at the Saufley Field Naval Auxiliary Air Station, Pensacola, Fla. Before entering service last June, Ensign Cherba was graduated from Baldwin-Wallace College.

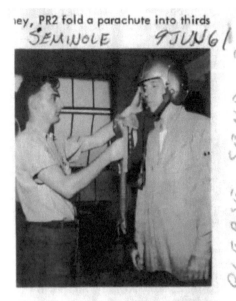

ey, PR2 fold a parachute into thirds
SEMINOLE 9 JUN 61
PLEASE SEND BAC...

M. D. Maione PR3, fitting ENS R. J. Cherba with a helmet and oxygen mask.

These and any paper like them were news releases by the Navy to our home town newspaper. I didn't know Mom cut these out. She did send me some, but I had to return them. Article to left was in base newspaper 'Seminole'

T-34 Mentor Saufley Field

T-28 Trojan Whiting Field WhitingField

F-9F8T Cougar Carrier Landing Training in Beeville TX

F-11F1 Tiger at Chase Field in Beeville TX a Supersonic Aircraft

Ensign R J Cherba upon the successful completion of Pre-Flight. Ensign(gold bar on shoulder board) commission awarded on October 21, 1960

This small trophy recognition of 1000 hours in the A4 at the time, was given to me by the Douglas representative, non military, who made the cruise with us. Douglas is the manufacture of the airplane. He could help and diagnose any problem we might be having with the a/c. He would also be able to order parts more quickly that were needed to get the airplane back in the air. I had a total of 636 A4 flights. First February 16,1962 and the last June 26,1966. This includes the time I spent in the

Naval Reserve VA-811 in Minneapolis MN.

This is the 1960-TR 3 that I bought when I completed Pre-Flight, commissioned as an Ensign and started drawing a real paycheck. So that is how I got around to the different training airports.

This picture taken on one of the vary rare times that I had the top up. In CA I always had the top down. When I had a musical gig, my drum set would fit in the car. I had a back bonnet rack which allowed me to tie down items that didn't fit inside. I believe this might have been taken overlooking Lake Superior. I felt like a race car driver whenever I got behind the wheel.

USS Antietam

My first flight in the F-9F8T was July 17, 1961 at Chase Field, in Beeville TX. Here I got 95 training flights. Also my first 6 carrier landings aboard the

USS Antietam on October 3,1961. Which was cruising in the Gulf of Mexico.

WINGS OF LEGACY

Last F-9 flight Nov.1,1961, From here we stayed at Chase field and transitioned to the F-11. A fighter. 23 Training flights and 25 hours. No carrier landings. But we did get to fire live ammo at a towed banner. Last F-11 flight was November 24, 1961.

I was designated a Naval Aviator

November 29,1961.Chase Field TX.

I had 8 more F9F flights here. Last one on January 28,1961.

Then went to NAS Lemoore CA and VA-125, another training squadron where we started flight training in the A-4D Skyhawk.

This would be the A/C that I would fly for the rest of my Navy career.

Ensign Richard Cherba

WINGS OF GOLD

This is the landing mirror system that projects a glide slope for the airplanes to follow to the flight deck. The LSO (Landing Signal Officer) stands on the stern (back) of the ship to monitor and if necessary help guide the pilot aboard.

This is the A-4C. Skyhawk. Made by Douglas Sometimes referred to as the "Scooter" also
"Scooter", "Kiddie Car", "Bantam Bomber", "Tinker Toy Bomber", "Mighty Midget"

NAS Lemoore 1-2-62

January 3, 1962,Two weeks after I got my wings I had to be in NAS Lemoore CA. A new base built in 1961. Attached to VT-125 a training squadron for the A-4, in the San Joaquin Valley, Out in the middle of nowhere. 40 miles south of Fresno CA. But it was home. From January 19-28,1962, I flew the F-9F for 8 more flights.

Started A-4 training February 16, 1962.

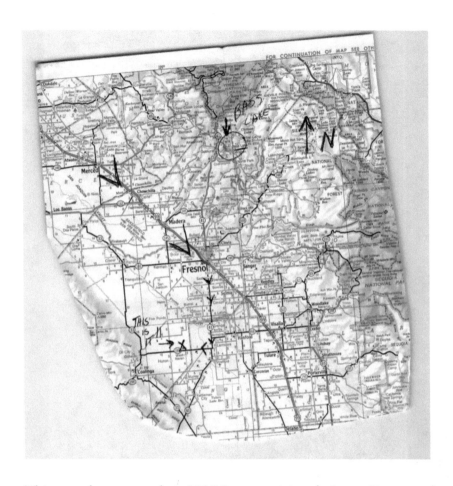

This map shows you where NAS Lemoore is in relation to Fresno and Bass Lake.

Lemoore-Fresno 38 miles/ 40 min.

Lemoore-Bass Lake 85 miles/ 1h 36 min.

Lemoore-Fallon Nevada 392 miles/6 1/2 hrs.

Reno-Fallon Nevada 63 miles/1 hr 6 minutes.

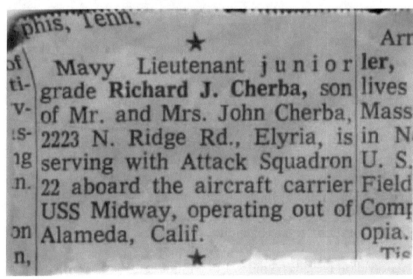

RICHARD CHERBA

December 1, 1960?

December 23, 1960

RICHARD CHERBA

December 23, 1960

RICHARD CHERBA

September 6, 1961

WINGS OF LEGACY

1-20-62

SAN DIEGO'S FAVORITE PROHIBITION—
—DAZE NIGHT SPOT UNIQUE
Open Wed. - Thurs. - Fri. - Sat. - Sun.
8:00 p.m. - 2:00 a.m.

Featuring —
- Complete Charlie Chaplin Movies
- Hot Banjo — Rinky Tink Piano
- Roaring Audience fun type music
- Wooden Nickles — Peanut Shells
- Happy Hour — 8 p.m. - 9 p.m.
  During Silent Movies
- Mixed Drinks - Draft Beer
- Wed. Night - Ladies Nite
- Thur. & Sunday — "Giggle" Hour

*We don't care wat Capone says—
We ain't movin' from dis place.*

This is a 1960s membership card. Many of these around the country. In 1960 this one was in San San Diego. Banjos, beer, food, sing a long, maybe peanuts. A fun place.

This is the bike that I bought. My friend got one also. We took them on a 40 mile round trip ride to Coalinga in the foot hills of the coastal range on the West side of the San Joaquin valley and came back with sore butts! Seats too small. Paul has this bike now. I have had it all these years.

RICHARD CHERBA

COMPETIZIONE

This is the one I got ↓

FRAME: 20" 3/4 - 22" 3/4 - 24" 1/2. High quality double butted steel tubing. Lugs, rear stays, fork head and front tips, heavily chrome plated. Flamboyant colors with chrome decorations. HANDLEBAR: «Ambrosio» special alloy racing bend and adjustable stem with plastic tape and plugs. BRAKES: «Universal» mod. 61 special alloy center Pull with alloy hooded levers white rubber. RIMS: High pressure 27 x 1.1/4" special alloy. TIRES: White sidewall 27 x 1.1/4", butyl tubes and Schraeder valves. SPOKES: Butted rustless. HUBS: «Campagnolo» record high flange, quick release. CHAINWHEEL: Special triple alloy sprocket 45 - 49 - 53. CHAIN: «Regina Extra» 1/2 x 3/32 pitch. FREEWHEEL: «Regina Extra» five sprocket 13 to 24. DERAILLEUR: «Campagnolo» Gran Sport 10 speed gear front changer. PEDALS: Special racing chrome plated steel. SADDLE: Unica black plastic racing model. EQUIPMENT: «Cornez» toe clips and straps, air pump. BIANCHI COLOURS: Flamboyant red Flamboyant blue Bhight black.

NEWS OF THE VALL[EY]

McClatchy Newspapers Service

The Fresno Bee, Fresno, Cal., Fri., Feb. 9, 1962

Lemoore Pilots Test Water Tight Suits In Far Pacific

ABOARD THE CORAL SEA WITH THE 7TH FLEET — These men are not trying to express the concept of hands across the ocean, nor are they doing a communal cartwheel, nor have they flipped their collective lid. All are pilots from Attack Squadron 153 (VA-153) which flew here recently from the Lemoore Naval Air Station in California and are enjoying the pleasant task of testing what it would feel like to be pooped in a "poopie" suit after plopping in the ocean.

Although they bear broad grins, the men know the test has very serious undertones, for if some day they should find themselves in the deep blue sea, MK4 exposure suits may save their lives.

These newly made old model suits (affectionately called "poopie") were tested for water tightness in the Philippine Islands at the NAS Cubi Point bachelor officers' quarters pool. The suits, in addition to being designed to keep men afloat, are lined for protection against the cold and are worn when the water is below 59 degrees.

It is expected they will be a welcome addition in the cold climes of Japan.

VA-153 is part of Carrier Air Group 15 presently attached to the attack carrier Coral Sea.

RICHARD CHERBA

Blue Angel Goes For Simple Life: Bossing Jet Unit

By Ron Taylor
Fresno Bee staff writer

LEMOORE NAVAL AIR STATION — Inside the Tiger jet cockpit a pilot, his right arm straining against the controls, calls to the three other blue jets packed tight around him:

"Diamond roll."

In cadence the answers come back: "Doug." "Bill." "Ken."

The tight formation — its wings overlapping 14 feet — flashes in over the crowd and the leader speaks again:

"Diamond roll . . . up we go . . . okay." The "okay" is a command.

Below thousands of persons stand in awe as the four supersonic jets scream up and over, moving in dramatic precision as if controlled by one pilot.

In effect they are controlled by one pilot. Until recently that flier was Commander Zeb Knott, leader of the Blue Angels.

But, for the first time in three and a half years, Commander Knott will be standing with the crowds May 30th, as this famed navy flight team puts on its aerial ballet over this station.

For Commander Knott is now a student at LNAS. He's assigned to Attack Squadron

Continued on page 4-B, col. 1

NEW ROUTINE — Commander Zeb Knott, right, with 19 years of flying plus leadership of the famed Blue Angels behind him, gets pointers from Commander O. L. Dolphin at Lemoore Naval Air Station on flying the Skyhawk. Bee Photo

1955
Richard John
Cherba

Front view of the A4 showing the external fuel tanks. These could be jettisoned if not needed anymore or if it would be part of a planned mission. But they could also be refueled in the air by another airplane that was a tanker. As long as our probe could fit in the basket. The A4, A3 and the Air Force had refueling a/c. They would refuel the SR-71, B-52s. Flying on a long flight say over the Atlantic, you could refuel on a planned meeting point. In the middle of the Atlantic.

RICHARD CHERBA

These were the totals at the end of my training.

RICHARD CHERBA

Seattle World's Fair   April 30, 1962

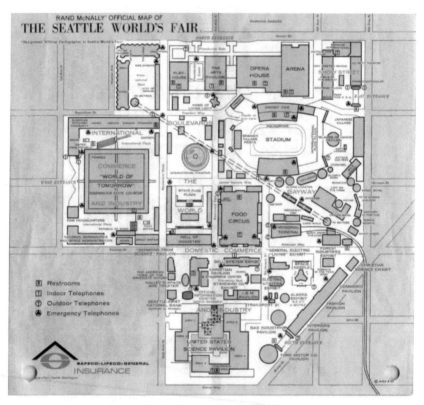

Seattle World's Fair - April 30, 1962

My Mom also saved some of the envelopes that the letters came in. There are only 12. They provided Mom and Dad my location at the time the letter was mailed. So throughout the book the date sequence could not be in exact date order.

Navy May 9, 1962 Fallon Nevada

Navy May 15, 1962 Fallon Nevada

Navy October 4, 1962 USS RANGER CVA-61

Navy November 2, 1962 USS Kearsarge CVS-33

RICHARD CHERBA

LTjg R J CHERBA
CVA-19
c/o FPO
SAN FRANCISCO, CALIF.

AIR   MAIL

MR. + MRS. JOHN CHERBA
2223 N. RIDGE RD
ELYRIA 7
OHIO

AIRMAIL

Navy December 4, 1962 USS Hancock CVA-19

YELLOWSTONE PARK COMPANY
Lake Hotel
Yellowstone Park, Wyoming

FISHING
ST

MR + MRS. JOHN CHERBA
2223 N. RIDGE RD
ELYRIA 7
OHIO   44038

Navy August 24, 1963 Yellowstone National Park

Navy November 10, 1963 USS Midway CVA-41

Navy November 22, 1963 Honolulu HI

RICHARD CHERBA

Navy December 10, 1963 USS Midway CVA-41

Navy December 26, 1963 Hong Kong

Navy January 4, 1964 USS Midway CVA-41

Navy March 15, 1964 USS Midway CVA-41

The date on this photo is Aug 1961. I did make a visit after I got my Wings. Mom wrote a note and made a comment about what little light there was that morning I left to take the photo. When I did start my journey to CA, I headed for the famous Highway 66. So the pictures/cards that follow are of the places I stopped along the way. It was like a vacation, sort of. Always wanted to visit Las Vegas and did stop there also. Played some games. This picture was taken in our front yard facing the house.

Got to Lemoore with only $5.00 left over from

Las Vegas for gas! Nice accommodations in the BOQ (Bachelor Officer Quarters). Motel type building with private rooms on both sides of the building and your own exterior entrance. A shared bathroom with the pilot on the other side. He was to become a very close and personal friend. Everett Alvarez.

I had orders to San Diego and survival school. O What fun that was.

My initial orders were to an A4 training Squadron VA-125. A training squadron where I would learn to fly the A4. Upon completion of the syllabus here I was given orders to VA-144 to report June 3, 1961. VA-144 was scheduled to deploy aboard the USS Constellation CVA-64 to The Western Pacific and Vietnam from 5 May 1964 to 1 February 1965. Everett was assigned to the same squadron. So we went through A4 training together. Neither of us had reported to the squadron yet, I don't think. During this time we both were about ready to be promoted to Lieutenant Jr Grade. Adding a 1/2 bar for a full 1-1/2 bar insignia. I was promoted on April 23, 1962. During this time period we met a couple from Hanford CA, just a few miles from base. they told us about a cabin they owned on Bass Lake about 1/2 way to Yosemite National Park, Some of us went up to see it. Well, we rented the lower apartment June 24, '62. 6 of us.

We could use it whenever we had no duties. It was one large room with kitchen and 6 beds. One of the guys had a ski boat and we had a dedicated dock. This is where I learned how to slalom ski and we did a lot of skiing when we were there. The cabin was a great place to relax. And drink beer!

The guys 1 guest,?, Me,Everett, Howie, Ralph-guest

These were the docks near our place. Not far from here was a bar that we went to. Typical of any resort with liquid refreshments and food.

The Falls Tavern was a bar with food and a small band on weekends. I got to know the band and the drummer, Roger Simonian. He allowed me to sit in once in a while and even play for him when he had other engagements. That was a whole lot of fun. A few of us went to the "Little Church in the Pines". Their choir was very small, 1 male, 10 women. The Pastor asked us if we would like to sing in it and we did. So we had 3 or 4 parts. That was in July 1962.

It is customary when you get promoted to throw a wetting down party. Everett had one in August. There was a lot of drinking, a party atmosphere. I decided to go to the cabin. It was late at night. So off I went. Well the roads are all twisty, tight hairpin turns. And in some spots the asphalt had bunched like a washboard, because of the daytime heat and traffic. I was wearing my leather flight jacket. As I was going around one of the tight turns, Andretti style, the car started to turn over on the left side. I laid over in the passenger seat and over I went. The car landed on its top and my left arm, on the elbow. Gas was leaking out of the tank which was behind the rear seats. Heard voices from people that were driving towards Yellowstone. Many gathered and lifted the car off of me. I stood up shaking my left arm, numb. The crowd was amazed that I was not dead, but walking around. I did not lose consciousness. I returned to the base the next morning. Checked in sick bay. The doctor decided that I needed to go to the Oakland Naval Hospital in Oakland CA. The doctors told me that there was not any medicine or surgery that would heal this injury. It would have to heal on its own.

The diagnosis was a severed radial nerve that controlled movement in the hand.would have to wear a removable brace until it healed. Needless to say I was off flight status.

I could not raise my hand from the wrist. This changed a lot of things. The accident was on July 31,1962.

I received temporary orders August 8, 1962 back to VA 125, the training squadron until my injury was healed enough to return to flying again. I did a lot of squadron duty of the day (SDO). And attended a few schools,

like Justice, weapons and ?.

With some time off, Roger and I took a trip to Las Vegas for a little fun. We stopped at Hoover Dam and took the tour. Restored car. They did a great job.

Me and Roger at Hoover Dam

You may have noticed the contraption on my left wrist. This is the removable brace that I was to wear until my nerve healed. The ends of the nerve had to meet together on their own.

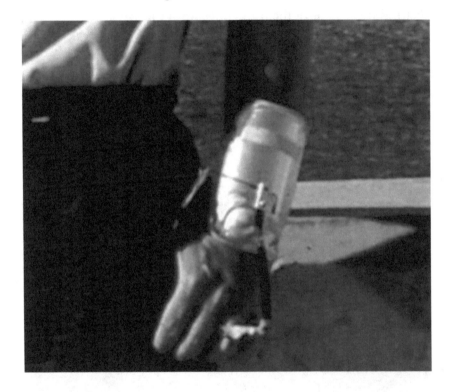

This is the device on my left wrist. It was a half metal shell that I could strap onto the arm with 2 straps. The black item reached up like a fishing pole, at an angle up. Attached at the end was a rubber band that was attached to a bar beneath the fingers. I could force my hand down and the band would allow it to come up. This was my problem. I could not raise my hand up. It all worked. I took it off when I water skied. No Problem. Even learned to slalom.

I visited Oakland a few times and was finally cleared for flying duty. During the time that my injury was healing, Mom and Dad came out from OH for a visit. I was very happy that they made the long drive to see me. I was able to get some time off and we visited a few parks.

Pictures are of some of them and not sure of the dates.

The car was a '55 or '56 Oldsmobile ?, 4 door, hardtop. I had to convince Dad to buy it. It had the latest electric gadget available at the time. A beam on the dash connected to a foot peddle that would dim the cars head lights. Wow! I don't think Dad needed too much convincing. The car that we had was a '49 Plymouth that I mentioned in my College letters.

The photo on top was in Yosemite. Bottom I don't know. Maybe Disneyland.

NAS Alameda CA was a seaport in Alameda by Oakland. The Navy ships would usually leave and return here from cruise. If we had liberty, we would usually head over to San Francisco and Broadway where there was a lot of activity. One of bars was the Red Garter. As you can see 6 banjos, lots of beer, food, and peanuts. Sing-a-long

San Francisco had a lot of entertainment on North Beach. Broadway. One night on liberty we werelooking for a place maybe to have another beer. We came across the Condor Club and the musical duo, Righteous Brothers who were appearing. there. Some of my favorite music of the time.

The music was great. Now all of a sudden from the ceiling there came a dancer. Carol Doda. Well she was topless. I had never heard of her. Later I found out that she was the first woman to get a silicon breast implant.

From Google, here is more information.

RICHARD CHERBA

The Condor Club in North Beach was world-famous for its star stripper, Carol Doda, who died in 2015 at age 78. Carol Doda made history not only as San Francisco's first topless dancer, but also as the nation's first to do it legally.

The club opened in 1958 and primarily operated as a music venue, putting on acts including Bobby Freeman, The Righteous Brothers and Sly Stone. Located at the corner of Broadway and Columbus Avenue

The Condor Club nightclub is a striptease bar or topless bar in the North Beach section of San Francisco, California The club became famous in 1964 as the first fully topless nightclub in America, featuring the dancer Carol Doda wearing a monokini. Needless to say, but we might have had another beer. don't remember if she sang.

Ernst ties wear remarkably well in an uncommon variety of situations.

I would like to explain some things. A lot of the information that is between these pages are from a few places. I used google once in awhile. The dates came from slides where some had dates stamped on the frame or non at all. And it also mattered when they would be developed. Some were b/w prints from the very early years. Some did or not have info on them. I got some info from my Navy folder called "junk". This folder contained all sorts of multiple copies of orders, awards and some physical records. Folder about 2-3 inches thick. Some info from my pilot Logbook. My memory is now about 61 years old. A lot of things that I had long forgotten or really didn't recall that particular activity at all.So you will encounter dates, etc that seem not to coincide with the actual subject or conflict with other notes. I did as well as I could and frankly spent too much time on trying to make the date chronology work. Anyway, here it is. I do hope that you enjoy the book anyway. I think you will enjoy reading about the shipboard life and the activities. Thanks, Dick.

I was returned to flying status on October 3,1962 and did a lot of catching up on some flying. Renewed my instrument rating and did some carrier work. I got orders to a different squadron, VA 22. They were on the Midway and just coming back from a WestPac cruise, Aug 15,1959-Mar 25,1960 and now starting a training cycle to prepare for the 1964 cruise on the USS Midway. The actual dates for our cruise.

would be Nov.8,1963, return May 26, 1964.

RICHARD CHERBA

The actual dates for our cruise. Nov 8, 1963-May 26, 1964. The following would be the training cycle for the August 1964-February 1965 cruise. I left in Apr '65.

Training schedule.

ATTACK SQUADRON TWENTY TWO
c/o Fleet Post Office
San Francisco, California
(96601)

5 August 1964

EXECUTIVE OFFICER'S NOTES – CONUS NO 1

As indicated in the last set of notes issued while deployed in WESTPAC, CONUS versions of the notes would be issued from time to time. This is the first.

NOTE 1. As this goes to press a number of squadron personnel are slaving very diligently in the E. M. Club dining room taking their advancement in rating tests. I want to wish them all the best of luck and I hope each one will see his name on the forthcoming advancement listing. A disturbing facet of this advancement business though is that I have a list of 19 squadron men on my desk who were eligible with respect to time in service, time in rating and other basic criteria for the August exams and they did not complete all preparations. Each man should try every time he can for an advancement. Lets see everyone that is eligible try in February.

NOTE 2. The CONUS training cycle appears to be reasonably firm now and even though I feel fairly certain the word has been passed around I would like to list the schedule.

1 – 16 August 1964	Lemoore Training
18– 19 August 1964	ADMAT Inspection
19– 30 August 1964	Lemoore training- include Bullpup firing
1 – 7 September 1964	Lemoore Training
8 – 25 September 1964	Fallon Deployment
26-30 September 1964	Lemoore Training
1 – 7 October 1964	Lemoore Training
8 Oct – 8 November 1964	Deployed in USS Midway (CVA-41) for MIDPAC (Pineapple cruise) and WEPTRAEX (Weapons Training Exercise)
9 – 30 November 1964	Lemoore Training
1 – 31 December 1964	Lemoore Training (Probable Christmas leave periods from 17-26 December and 26 Dec-5 Jan)
1 – 7 January 1965	Lemoore Training
8 – 25 January 1965	STRIKE EX (Strike Training Exercise in USS MIDWAY (CVA-41)
26-31 January 1965	Lemoore Training
1 – 7 February 1965	Lemoore Training
8 February (About)	Presently scheduled WESTPAC Cruise date – Deployment in USS MIDWAY (CVA-41)

NOTE 3. In the above schedule note the frequency of the word "training". That doesn't just mean pilot training even though that is where the visible evidence seems to point. Each squadron member must be refreshed on old skills, learn new ones and increase his individual readiness to carry out the squadron mission. Don't waste any time at all in the few months we have. Make all the training count.

1

NOTE 4. Voting is a right and priviledge granted every United States citizen who is 21 or more years old. A preliminary survey indicates a number of personnel who could be voting in the November election have not as yet mailed an absentee voter application. To have a part in your countries government you must vote. When contacted by the Voting Officer, LTJG LEE, fulfill your responsibility by applying for a ballot and then on election day VOTE for the man and principle of your choice. California residents have until 10 September to register. The Voting Officer has the information for other states.

NOTE 5. Use of vulgar language seems to be on the upswing, throughout the squadron areas. Normally thoughts are expressable without insertion of from one to five cuss words in each sentence. Run a mental check regarding the language you have been using here at work. Lets all make an effort to cut down on vulgar terms.

NOTE 6. A few other items to think about are mentioned below. Admiral Arleigh A. Burke said in August 1955 - "<u>Tactical advances and the possibilities of the nuclear age not withstanding it is men who will eternally remain as the one essential ingredient to successfully maritime operations</u>". You, as members of a naval aviation squadron, are the essential ingredients which make this unit tick. Your every day performance of assigned duties along with your attitude, sense of cooperation and ability to work together are the factors getting the job done. How well the job is accomplished depends on the way each one of you take it upon yourself to accept responsibilities, to give each job the extra effort that ensures timely completion and to positively assure all details are accomplished properly. The majority of squadron personnel demonstrate these factors in an examplory fashion and hence the "E" award along with an outstanding reputation. It is good from time to time, however, to mentally review your own performance. Ask yourself how it can be improved. And too, how do you stand personally in your concepts and practices of basic moral laws so vital to good human relations. Are you doing all you can toward enhancing human dignity, natural rights, national and individual moral conscience, recognition of obligations of justice, patriotism, loyalty, honesty, honor, decency, truth, reverence for God and similar virtues. Your shipmates depend upon you for the best of qualities in each of these virtues.

NOTE 7. LT Paul GRAFTON has recently joined the squadron after completing A4 training with VA-125. LT GRAFTON will assume the duties as Aircraft Contol Officer in the Maintenance Department.

C. E. Dechow
C. E. DECHOW
CDR USN
Executive Officer, VA-22

2

RICHARD CHERBA

October 21, 1962

December 1962

We went through Hawaii many times for various reasons. On different ships. Not always on Midway.

Sometimes we would have land operations at NAS Barber's Point. December 16, 1963 USS Handcock.

RICHARD CHERBA

November 23, 1963 Hawaii Blow Hole

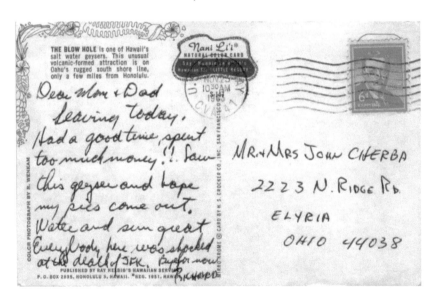

August 1963

RICHARD CHERBA

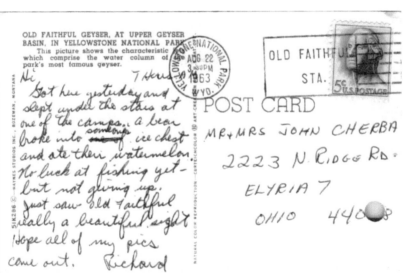

August 22, 1963 Read card about my close call with a bear. True story.
I caught 6 trout, I gave away. No way to cook.

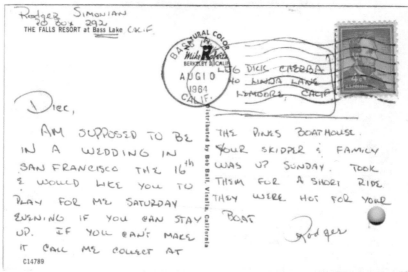

The Falls Resort. This is where I met Roger. He allowed me to sit in with the band and play for him. He would call me occasionally to play for him at a job if he had a conflict. We had some fun together.

August 10, 1964

Top: our dock at the cabin at Bass Lake
Bottom: our rental.

> Hi, 19 AUG.
> Just a few lines to say hello. Got home Sat night. It was a long 2½ weeks. Last night went to see "How the West was Won" in Cinerama. It was a very good picture.
>
> Leaving in a few minutes for Yellowstone via Yosemite and Salt Lake City, so I will be writing from there. Then on the 30th will be heading for Hawaii for 3 wks. prob. 2 week ends in port. We will be in Hong Kong for Xmas this year. By for now!
> Love
> Richard

August 19, 1963

Mr & Mrs John Cherba
2223 N. Ridge Rd.
Elyria 7
Ohio 44038

Thanksgiving Dinner 1963
U.S.S. *Midway* CVA-41
Enroute Philippines From Hawaii

CAPTAIN L. E. HARRIS, USN
COMMANDING OFFICER

CDR. D. H. STINEMATES, USN
EXECUTIVE OFFICER

CDR. G. C. LEMMON, SC, USN
SUPPLY OFFICER

ENS. M. M. BERLOWSKI, SC, USNR
WARDROOM MESS CATERER

H. W. RILEY, SDCS, USN
CHIEF STEWARD

A Thanksgiving Prayer

O All-Good and All-Loving God, Who has blessed us with material abundance and bestowed upon us many spiritual graces, we render thanks unto Thee for this food and for all Thy gifts which we have received from Thy bounty.

As we recall our heritage of faith and freedom this Thanksgiving, we pray that Thou would enliven us with a spirit of sharing our blessings with others, and give us truly grateful hearts to praise Thee and thank Thee forever. Amen.

Wardroom Mess
Thanksgiving Day Dinner
1963

Canapes
Fresh Shrimp Cocktail

Iced Relish Tray	Salted Mixed Nuts
Sliced Tomato	Blue Cheese Dressing
Celery Soup	Toasted Saltines
Roasted Tom Turkey	Virginia Baked Ham
Corn Meal Dressing	Cider Sauce
Giblet Gravy	Cranberry Sauce
Candied Yams	Whipped Potatoes

Buttered Green Beans With Cauliflower
Hot Parkerhouse Rolls With Butter

Pumpkin Pie w/cream   Hot Mince Pie   Fruit Cake
Ice Cream
Coffee   Tea   Hot Chocolate   Fresh Milk
Assorted Candies

We spent time in San Diego, so made at least one visit to Tijuana, Mexico.
April 27, 1963

RICHARD CHERBA

August 12, 1963

USS Midway CVA-41   Under sail.

*One of these is a statue. Can you tell which one?
Called a shooter and the last person you see once he touches the deck with his right hand. These were taken on the USS Midway Museum, San Diego CA*

These photos were taken in 2018 on a family visit. The shooter would control your taxi to the catapult. The yellow shirts were the taxi directors on the flight deck and there were many shirt colors on the deck with various jobs. The catapult consists of a track, or slot, built into the flight deck, below which is a large piston or shuttle that is attached through the track to the nose gear of the aircraft. Fastened with a breakaway bolt. A blast fence would raise behind to deflect the jet blast.

The cat shot is subject to a few things, your weight, shooter confirming the settings from some men that were located in the catwalk adjacent to the flight deck. Your job was to sweep the cockpit with the control stick to make sure that the controls were free and clear, final instrument check and when all was ready you gave the shooter a snappy salute. He would then assume this position, touch the deck, the signal for the crew to push the button and gradually off you went for an end speed of around 170 mph. The USS Hancock had a hydraulic cat, which meant you were up to speed almost immediately. You were off the ship quickly either way.

A catapult bridle, is attached to the aircraft and the catapult shuttle with a breakaway bolt.

During our turn-around time we had been at sea many times. Mostly getting refresher landings and spending various times at Fallon NV. It is located 60 miles East of Reno NV. The only entertainment here was a pool table, maybe a ping pong table and a shuffle board. Of course, this was NV and just off base was a bar, Mas, that offered gambling. If you could barrow a car you could make your way into Reno, "The Biggest Little City in the World".

This is a bombing range where we practiced various types of bombing. The ordnance we used were practice bombs, MK-76. These had a detonation charge that would leave a smoke signal to allow the spotters at the targets to tell you where your bomb fell. You could try to do better on the next run. There were many deployments to Fallon of various times. Maybe a two week deployment and days where we could fly three hops a day.

We were preparing for our Far East cruise. Scheduled to leave the beginning of November 1963.

If I was a junior officer in the Squadron, I had to drive to Fallon. I drove the Skippers car once. It was in the Winter. The car had no heat. On the way back to Lemoore, the radiator sprung a leak. By luck we were in Lake Tahoe. It was repaired with stop leak and a toothpick. The Skipper drove that car, Hudson, for a long time, sold car with tooth-pick in it.

Fastest Gun in the West

There are 887 armor-piercing 20-mm cannon shells visible in this picture, a little more than ⅓ the complete load for the three pods under this Navy Skyhawk A-4 jet fighter. The A-4 carries the new HIPEG gun system developed by the Hughes Tool Co. at Culver City, Calif. The system fires at the rate of 12,600 rounds a minute, which would exhaust the shells shown in about four seconds.

This is some of the ordnance that we can carry. Fuel tanks wing and center fuselage can hold 1000 lbs of fuel each.

This is one of ours. Note the Redcock logo on the fuselage and the 'E'. Each wing has a 250 lb bomb on it and the center rack has a fuel tank with 1000 lbs of fuel on it.

The USS Midway left Alameda NAS (Naval Air Station) for HI on November 8, 1963. About a 6 day sail. We did some flying around HI. There is always a rescue helicopter or 2 when we have air operations.

Left HI on November 25th for a 12 day sail to Subic Bay in the Philippines. We took a short cut through the middle of Luzon instead of going around the North side of Luzon. We did some flying there also. Arrived December 7th. Left December 13 to go to Hong Kong. Christmas in Hong Kong.

While in HI, We had air operations and inspections and of course some time off to enjoy the Island.

During our time in port we learned of the assassination of President Kennedy. The news came over the speaker system in the Navy PX. Think Walmart. Doing some last minute shopping before leaving HI.

Here is an excerpt from the '63-'64 cruise book.

RICHARD CHERBA

The tragedy of the untimely death of our President shrouded the in-port period at Pearl, and as the senior ship present, we were obliged to render honors as the saluting battery broke the hovering silence with each of its twenty-one reports.

Thereafter, the homage devoted to the passing, the Arizona memorial took on a new meaning as the National Ensign was lowered to its half-mast position.

This is one of the dinners we tried.

The Luau Story

Many countries have their own traditional get-togethers accompanied by entertainment and a feast of native delicacies. Hawaii has one of the most exotic and unusual ... THE LUAU.

AHAAINA or "the gathering of friends to eat" was the ancient Hawaiian word for this event; later, LUAU meaning "leaf of the taro" became the common expression used by the early missionaries and sea captains.

At Queen's Surf the luau is not merely a means of satisfying hunger. It is an unhurried affair, a meeting of friends, a time of laughter, of music, of entertainment. The guests gather at sunset in the Polynesian Garden overlooking the water at Waikiki. Tables covered in TAPA, TI leaves and island flowers are arranged under the palm trees and as evening falls the torches are lit and the luau begins.

The Queen's Surf Luau
NATIVE FEAST

EVERY SUNDAY AT 6:30 P.M.

PLUS THURSDAYS DURING JULY AND AUGUST
$8.50 including all taxes

6:30 to 7:15 p.m. Highballs or Polynesian Rum Punch and entertainment.

7:15 to 9:00 P.M. THE LUAU
Authentic Hawaiian food cooked in the IMU and reenactment of ancient Hawaiian rituals ...
Presenting the most outstanding entertainers in the Islands in songs and dances of Hawaii.

FOR RESERVATIONS:
See your travel agent or telephone Queen's Surf — 937387.

The Luau Menu

PUAA KALUA (Baked Pork) ... Whole pig cooked in the underground oven or "Imu". The "Imu" is Polynesia's original pressure cooker where the red hot "pohakus" (rocks) make the succulent pig "papaa" (crispy brown).
LOMI LOMI SALMON ... Lomi Lomi means kneaded or massaged in Hawaiian. Lomi Lomi Salmon is King Salmon kneaded with the fingers to remove the bones, then chopped, mixed with fresh tomatoes and green onions and served ice cold.
MOA LUAU (Chicken with taro leaves) ... tender Island chicken cooked with taro tops (Hawaiian Spinach) and coconut cream, then served in half a coconut shell.
I'A LUAWELA (Fish baked in ti leaves) ... a tasty piece of butterfish is first placed on a bed of luau leaves along with a small cube of pork for flavor, then wrapped in ti leaves and cooked in the "Imu".
POI (Taro root pounded into a paste) ... It is the staple food of the Hawaiians, taking the place of bread, and is traditionally eaten with one or two fingers in accompaniment with spicy native dishes.
PAAKAI (Hawaiian rock salt) ... as in ancient times this salt is the residue of evaporated ocean spray and is scraped from rock cavities along the coast line. Sprinkle on your poi.
HALAKAHIKI (Pineapple luau style) ... standing pineapples which appear whole and uncut but which are hollowed, cored, cut into long spears and reassembled with the top as a lid—one of the desserts of the Hawaiian luau.
MAIA KALUA (Banana cooked in imu).
HAUPIA (Arrowroot, coconut and pineapple pudding) ... served on a ti leaf.
BANANA MUFFINS ... homemade in our kitchen from ripe Island bananas. A modern Hawaiian delicacy.
FRESH COCONUT CAKE ... a butter and egg cake with marshmallow and freshly grated coconut on top.
HOT COFFEE ... An American touch.
HAWAIIAN RUM PUNCH ... as many cups as you wish of our own blend of exotic Hawaiian fruit juices and old "Whaling Ship Rum".

RICHARD CHERBA

'JUMBO' — the largest and most luxurious floating restaurant in the world, where you can enjoy, among others, delicious fresh sea-food and dim-sum with courteous service.

POST CARD

JUMBO FLOATING RESTAURANT
SHUM WAN ABERDEEN, HONG KONG.

PLACE STAMP HERE

JF

ADDRESS

I am not sure that we ate here. It was a huge structure floating on the water. Part of the menu was to pick out the live fish that they would prepare for your dinner. Of course, a large sea food menu.

The Jumbo was closed March 2020. On 14 June 2022, the Jumbo Floating Restaurant was being towed Cambodia to await a new operator. While transiting in the South China Sea, it experienced bad weather and capsized near the Paracel Islands on 19 June 2022. It sank.

AVIATORS TAKEN PRISONER OF WAR

Date - Aviator - Aircraft - Squadron - Cause - Highest Award

Date	Aviator	
5 Aug 64	LTJG Everett Alvarez Jr. – A-4C – VA-144 – AAA	
3 Apr 65	LCDR Raymond Arthur Vohden – A-4C – VA-216 – AAA	
20 Apr 65	LT Philip Neal Butler – A-4C – VA-22 – OWN ORDNANCE	
2 Jun 65	LT John Bryan McKamey – A-4E – VA-23 – AAA	
24 Aug 65	LTJG Richard Marvin Brunhaver – A-4C – VA-22 – A/C MALFUNCTION	
26 Aug 65	LTJG Edward Anthony Davis – A-1H – VA-152 – AAA	
9 Sep 65	CDR James Bond Stockdale – A-4E – CAG-16 – AAA	
10 Sep 65	LCDR Wendell Burke Rivers – A-4E – VA-155 – AAA	
13 Nov 65	CDR Harry Tarleton Jenkins Jr. – A-4E – VA-163 – AAA	
22 Dec 65	LTJG Wendell Reed Alcorn – A-4C – VA-36 – AAA	
23 Dec 65	LTJG William Leonard Shankel – A-4C – VA-94 – AAA	
1 Feb 66	LTJG Dieter Dengler – A-1H – VA-145 – AAA – ESCAPED	
7 Feb 66	LCDR Render Crayton – A-4E – VA-56 – AAA	
17 Mar 66	LTJG Frederick Charles Baldock Jr. – A-4C – VA-94 – SAM	
20 Mar 66	CDR James Alfred Mulligan Jr. – A-4C – VA-36 – AAA	
25 Mar 66	LTJG Bradley Edsel Smith – A-4C – VA-76 – AAA	
20 Apr 66	CDR John Abbott – A-4C – VA-113 – DAP	
15 Jun 66	LCDR Theodore Frank Kopfman – A-4E – VA-55 – AAA	
17 Jun 66	LTJG Paul Edward Galanti – A-4C – VA-216 – AAA	
15 Jul 66	LT James Joseph Connell – A-4E – VA-55 – AAA – DAP	
28 Jul 66	ENS George Palmer McSwain Jr. – A-4E – VA-164 – SAM	
4 Oct 66	LCDR John Douglas Burns – A-4C – VA-22 – SAM	
12 Oct 66	LT Robert Deane Woods – A-1H – VA-25 – AAA	
20 Oct 66	LTJG Frederick Raymond Purrington – A-4C – VA-172 – AAA	
1 Nov 66	LT Alan Russell Carpenter – A-4E – VA-72 – AAA	
21 Dec 66	LTJG Danny Ellroy Glenn – A-4C – VA-144 – AAA	
5 Jan 67	LCDR Richard Allen Stratton – A-4E – VA-192 – OWN ORDNANCE	
13 Jan 67	LTJG Michael Paul Cronin – A-4E – VA-23 – AAA	
11 Mar 67	CDR Ernest Melvin Moore Jr. – A-4E – VA-192 – SAM	
25 Apr 67	LT Charles David Stackhouse – A-4C – VA-76 – MiG	
6 May 67	LTJG Robert Earle Wideman – A-4E – VA-93 – AAA	
18 May 67	CDR Kenneth Robbins Cameron – A-4C – VA-76 – AAA – DAP	

18 May 67	
20 May 67	
26 May 67	
30 May 67	
31 May 67	
22 Jun 67	
30 Jun 67	
9 Jul 67	
14 Jul 67	
18 Jul 67	
31 Aug 67	
31 Aug 67	
4 Oct 67	
26 Oct 67	
26 Oct 67	
17 Nov 67	
22 Dec 67	
3 Jan 68	
5 Jan 68	
11 Jun 68	
24 Jul 68	
18 Sep 68	
23 Sep 68	
19 May 72	
27 May 72	
11 Jul 72	
6 Aug 72	
17 Aug 72	
25 Sep 72	
20 Dec 72	

AAA = ANTI-AIRCRAFT AR
SAM = SURFACE-TO-AIR
MiG = ENEMY AIRCRAFT
A/C = AIRCRAFT
DAP = DIED AS POW

RICHARD CHERBA

This list is on the Midway. Phil Butler and I were on the same night strike over Viet Nam. Phil was in the number 4 position when his ordinance malfunctioned and I did not know that until many years later. Phil wrote a book about his experiences. I left the Navy on May 25,1965. Skip Brunhaver became a POW after I had gone home. Everett Alvarez deployed with VA 144 on the USS Constellation. Everett was my roommate at the BOQ Lemoore.

This grease pencil board, no electronics yet, was located in Pri Fly located in the tower of the Midway, The Air Boss was in charge of running the flight operations and flight deck. This picture was taken in 2018 on one of my two return trips to visit the museum. I wanted you to take note of two names on this board. Brunhaver and Butler. These two VA-22 pilots never returned to the ship during Viet Nam. When you launch for a mission, your info was placed on this board and erased when you returned. Name, type A/C. side number and fuel on board. They became POWs in Viet Nam and never returned to the ship. Thus their names remain on the board. Only when released by the Vietnamese did they get to come home, not the ship but their home here in the USA. They were POWs Phil and Skip of 7-1/2 years and Everett 8-1/2 years.

From Internet about LTJG Richard (Skip) Brunhaver. VA-22's Lt. j.g. Richard Brunhaver was pulling out of a bombing run on a bridge when his flight control column froze on Aug. 24. His A-4 Skyhawk struck the treetops and caught fire as it slowly climbed. Forced to ejected, he was swiftly captured. Released from captivity in 1973, he spent more than seven years as a prisoner of war in Hanoi where he endured harsh treatment.

*This photo shows Skip, far left, at the Hanoi Hilton.
Skip passed away in 2023 after I wrote this.*

Just landed, notice black/white striped tailhook on rear of a/c.
The Midway angled deck. Just landed.

An A4 ready to give someone a drink refueling. The basket had fabric at opening so it opens with the wind. Allows for easier access with the probe. Hopefully! Might take a few tries. Tanker always airborne during launch and recovery operations.

Well dressed aviator. Steel toed boots to protect your toes in the event you have to eject. Helmet, O2, mask, stocked life vest, parachute harness, flight suit, also a tail hook (black/white rod).

This Philippine Christmas card was mailed before we left the islands.

I bought these postcards. Didn't visit any of these sights, but if did fly over Taal Lake and Volcano. I did fly over some other volcanos and could actually look directly into the caldron. Great place to roast marshmellows.

RICHARD CHERBA

MORO VINTAS — With colorful sails, these boats race across the Basilan Strait to the rich fishing grounds of the Sulu Sea.

P49728

Dist. by National Book Store, Manila, Philippines

TAAL LAKE AND VOLCANO — Published in Ripley's "Believe It or Not", this island within an island, a lake within a lake, is one of nature's wonders in the island of Luzon.

Dist. by National Book Store, Manila, Philippines

RICHARD CHERBA

MAYON VOLCANO
Legaspi City, Philippines
The most beautiful perfect cone among world-famous volcanoes. Erupted 30 times from 1616 to 1947.

Dist. by National Book Store, Manila, Philippines

PAGSANJAN FALLS — About 90 Kms. south of Manila, these falls in Pagsanjan, Laguna, are one of the country's top tourist attractions.

Dist. by National Book Store, Manila, Philippines

RICHARD CHERBA

THOUSAND HILLS OF CARMEN, BOHOL — These thousand hills on the flat plains of Bohol Province are one of its tourist attractions.

Dist. by National Book Store, Manila, Philippines

MORO WATCH TOWER IN THE ILOCOS — This tower is one of the numerous towers built during the early 17th and 18th centuries when Moro pirates raided early Christian settlements along coastal areas of the Ilocos.

Dist. by National Book Store, Manila, Philippines

A view of the commercial section of Baguio City, the summer capital of the Philippines.

Baugio is a summer resort. Navy drove Henry Papa, Warner Lee and me up there for a little R&R. 5 hrs one way, switchbacks all the way. Stayed at Camp John Hay Country Club. Played some golf. This where we bought some wood carvings. The visit to Baguio was about January 12, 1964

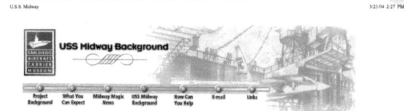

Midway Magic Factoids

During three tours of duty in the Tonkin Gulf, aircraft from the USS Midway downed the first three and last MiG in the Vietnam conflict.

The USS Midway was the first carrier to be "forward deployed" in a foreign country, sailing for 17 years out of Yokosuka, Japan.

The USS Midway played host to the dawn of naval missile warfare in 1947 when a captured German V-2 rocket was successfully launched from her deck and later detonated over the Atlantic Ocean.

Nearly 200,000 American veterans have served aboard the Midway in her 47 years of service.

The USS Midway literally was a "City at Sea," carrying a crew of 4,500, up to 70 aircraft and weighing more than 67,000 tons, fully loaded.

When operating at sea, the USS Midway was refueled every three days. She burned approximately 100,000 gallons a day.

When she was first built, the USS Midway's bow was open to the sea. It was enclosed in 1957 as part of a major overhaul.

Even in the absence of any major publicity effort, more than 5,000 people have signed up as potential Midway Magic visitors, volunteers, contributors and newsletter readers.

How popular is the Midway? In the three days before being "mothballed" in Seattle, more than 50,000 people visited her for a final look.

The Midway was named for the Battle of Midway, considered by many to be the turning point in the Pacific War. The movie by the same name was actually shot aboard the USS Lexington and USS Constellation.

Tourism industry experts predict as many as 700,000 people will visit Midway Magic in her first year of operation in San Diego.

These 4 pages will give you an idea of the history of what the Midway can carry. Ship is 1,001ft long. Beam. 258 ft, flight deck 4.02 acres. Statistics compare to today's cruise ships without a pool.

Since adding the Midway numbers, I found some others that you might be interested in. Some are repeats.

There's 2,000 feet of anchor chain aboard the USS Midway.
Each chain link weighs 130 pounds.
Anchors weigh 20 tons each.
The Midway is 1,001 feet long: 3+ football fields
The flight deck is 4.02 acres.
The catapult power is 0 to 170 mph in 3 seconds or less.

(An aircraft carrier does not have the space that an airport does, i.e., no runway. In order to get the planes airborn they are launched or catapulted into the air-0 to 170 mph in 3 seconds.)

The landing area within arresting wires is equal to the size of a tennis court.

one of three cables or arresting wires. The cables stretch up to 273 feet. The plane must stop by then otherwise it crashes. One vet I talked to, Bob, said that stress tests have shown landing on an aircraft carrier at night is more stressful than surprise attack. Bob had 1243 launches. He said you want to have equal number of landings. He did.)

The flight deck is 50 feet off the water.
The aircraft carrier draws a 35-foot draft under water.
4,300 crew worked to support 200 aviators: approx. 750 men/women in engineering; 225 cooks.

I toured the hangar deck with the berthing spaces, where they slept, and then went up the Island, which is like the air traffic control tower. I missed the second deck with the mess, food galley, sick bay and post office. According to someone who did visit that area, it is impressive.

10 tons of food per day
13,500 meals a day
10,500 cups of coffee at a time
4,500 pounds of beef per meal when served
3,000 pounds of potatoes per day
1,000 loaves of bread a day
650 pies when served

The aircraft carrier weighs 70,000 tons. I wonder if that is before or after a meal. Regardless, it was all rather interesting.

USS Midway by the Numbers

Flight Deck Operations
- Flight deck personnel during flight ops: 250
- 1,500 feet: total length of arresting wire on board
- 1,800 feet of anchor chain aboard
- 1,001 feet long: Over 3 football fields
- 340 feet the length of the runout when a plane lands
- 258 feet wide
- 220 feet to the top of the mast
- 4,000+ pad eyes on fight deck and hangar deck (to secure aircraft)
- 55 feet: elevation of flight deck off the water (today)
- 3½ inches of steel armor in the flight deck

Landing
- 45 seconds: the time between landings day time, 60 seconds at night
- Successful landings: 95% day, 88% at night
- Aviators had to be 12 feet off the deck as they passed the round-down in order to catch a wire
- The actual landing area for jets was about the size of a tennis court
- 100 landings: expected lifespan of flight deck arresting cables
- 1: number of landings more than 15 feet off centerline that would require the cable to be replaced

Launching
- Catapult power: 0 to 170 mph (150 knots) in 3 seconds or less
- 90 seconds between launches
- Catapult length: approx. 265 feet

Ship Structure
- 69,000 tons full load
- 190,000 pieces in the flight deck
- 4.02 acre flight deck
- 30,000 light fixtures
- 2,000 compartments
- 1,500 telephones
- 156 pounds: each anchor chain's link
- 20 tons: weight of each anchor
- 4 propellers: two 4-bladed props weigh 21.7 tons and are 18' 8" across. Two 5-bladed props weigh just 19.7 tons and measure 17' 6" across.
- 12 boilers and 4 high-pressure/low-pressure turbines
- 18 decks, equivalent of a 20-story building
- 35-foot draft under water in 1991. Today it's about 29 feet.

- Flight elevators: 130,000 pound capacity, up to flight deck in 15-20 seconds

Speed & Fuel
- Speed (approximate)
  o 33 knots = 38 miles per hour
- aircraft landing speed: 150 knots = 172 mph
- aircraft could land about every 45 seconds
- Midway went so fast you could water ski behind it
- 4 turbines produced a combined 212,000 horsepower
- 3.5 million gallons of ship & aviation fuel
- 100,000 gallons consumed daily in the ship's boilers.
- Fuel economy: approximately 260 gallons to the mile (or about 20 feet per gallon) at 15 knots
  o 900 gallons per mile at 30 knots

Crew
- Average sailor age: 19
- 200-300 aviators
- (90% of crew: 4,200-4,300 supported about 250 pilots)
- Approx. 650 men in engineering
- Approx. 225 cooks
- Approx. 30 corpsmen
- 40 commanding officers in 47 years
- 3 chaplains

Logistics
- 10 tons of food per day
- 13,000 meals a day
- 10,500 cups of coffee at a time
- 4,500 pounds of beef per meal when served
- 3,000 pounds of potatoes per day
- 1,000 loaves of bread a day
- 500 pies when served
- Desert Storm: 35,000-40,000 dozen eggs in route to Midway at any given point in time
- 198 pounds of dry laundry in each of 6 washing machines
- 1,725 the maximum rpm of the washing machines
- 350 degrees: maximum temperature of the washing machines
- 4,752 pounds of laundry could be washed every 12 hours
- 43,000 pounds of laundry per week
- 1,075 40-pound laundry bags weekly
- 2,000,000 pounds of laundry annually

- Food storage
  o 1 butcher shop
  o 2 bakeries
  o 1 vegetable prep room
  o 15 storerooms
  o 5 freezers

- 4 chill boxes
- Capacity
  - 70 tons of food
  - 10-11 tons consumed daily
  - 14,000 pounds of chicken
  - 14,400 pounds of grill steaks
  - 16,000 pounds of coffee
  - Daily cost of feeding crew in 1976: $10,000

Underway Replenishment
- 1-2 times per week
- Supply ship sailed alongside, about 150-200 feet from Midway
- Sailing at 10-15 knots
- 100 tons of dry cargo per hour
- Approx. 12,000 gallons/minute of fuel through 4 hoses

Other
- Parts inventory: 54,000 for aircraft, 36,000 for ship $85.6 million original cost
- 90 tons of blueprints to build in 1945. Equals the weight of about 35,500 reams of paper.
- $100 million in spare parts inventory
- $42 million monthly payroll
- 80,000 haircuts annually
- 280,000 gallons of freshwater produced daily

Note: Given Midway's long service, some statistics varied over the years. This list is representative overview (with some figures rounded off or approximated) of the USS Midway's service life.

Sources: Docent Manual, various USS Midway and U.S. Navy documents.

Updated Jan. 27, 2020

All of the carriers use steam to operate the catapult. Except 1, the USS Hancock, uses hydraulics

Difference- steam would be a gradual acceleration and the hydraulics would give it to you all at once. At times we did use the USS Hancock for carrier qual refresher.

The ship left the Philippines on December 13, 1963 on our way to Hong Kong. Where we arrived on Dec 21, 1963. Due to the ship's size, we had to anchor in the harbor and use a tender or one of the ship's life boats to go ashore. About a 45 minute trip. While in port we had the duty for one day. The ship provided a small crew in one of these life boats to guard the ship at night. It had to have one officer that could command a ship (designated by a star on the uniform shoulder board) , a chief and some sailors who actually ran the boat. The chief was the only person that had a side arm. This was a 4 hour watch and we just went around the ship to repel any intruders until our time was up. I think I had the midnight to 4 am watch.

While in port, the Chinese painted the hull.

Dan Gildner and I hung out together and we did a lot of sight seeing.

Dear Mom & Dad,   December 25, 1963

 The ship is anchored out so we have to catch a ferry every time we want to come in or go back. It's about a 45 minute boat ride. Tomorrow we decided to have breakfast in bed. Just for kicks! We act like the last of the big time spenders. The ship is anchored out so we have to catch a ferry every time we want to come in or go back. It's about a 45 minute boat ride.

   We leave her Sat. And our section has the duty Fri. So tomorrow is our last day in the city. We'll be heading back towards the Philippines. Enjoyed all the Xmas cards and also look forward to your letters. Bye for now. Going out to dinner to improve eating Chinese dishes with chopsticks. Getting pretty good, too!   Love, Richard

RICHARD CHERBA

Dec/26/1963

We left HK Dec 27, 1963 to return to Subic Bay. Arrived Jan 6, 1963. Left Jan 15, 1964 to Sasebo January 24, 1964. We would then sail further North to the cities of Beppu, Iwakuni, Yokosuka, and Atsugi. We did get to spend time in these cities, but not much.

From one of these cities, we did visit and get pictures of Nagasaki. This is one of the two cities where we dropped the Atomic Bomb. Took a train from Iwakuni to visit the other bombed city,

Hiroshima. Pics here also. I know we went to see the castle at Kobe. No pictures. I checked with my fellow aviator, Dan, and he didn't either. We really didn't have the cameras. So there are none. Both of these cities had great museums that showed the damage from the bomb.

On one of our visits to Atsugi and the ship was either at a pier or anchored, the squadron had to get an airplane to a repair facility. I was elected. The airplane was loaded with just enough gas to get me there. Which may have been about a 20 minute flight. Anyway, with no wind over the deck and a snappy salute off I went. So that went very well. At least I didn't end up in the water. I do not remember how I got back to Midway.

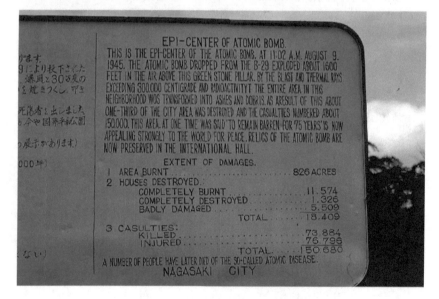

*We did get to visit the Nagasaki City Memorial.
This pillar was the target. We took a taxi tour.*

RICHARD CHERBA

NAGASAKI INTERNATIONAL CULTURAL HALL

This hall was built in the A-bombed area (Urakami) in Feburary 1955 as the monument in order to seek consolation for the A-bomb victims numbering more than 70,000. It is one of the typical buildings of Japan's modern architecture and has been introduced to various academic circles of the world.

1-st Floor : The memorial hall of this establishment occupies this floor, in which is placed a large globe, intended to mean world peace.

2-nd Floor : This floor has a conference-room, used for conferences and wedding ceremonies.

3-rd & 4 th Floors : These two floors ore taken up by the Nagasaki City Museum having historical materials contributing largely to Japan's modern history.

5-th Floor : This floor is devoted to the A-bomb, relics telling the visitors the tragedy of the century.

6-th Floor : This floor has a tea-room. (photographs and othe items are displayed.)

The rooftop offers an excellent view of the city, enabling the visitors to see how Nagasaki has been reconstructed.

The auditorium has a capacity of 1,000 persons, and is used for academic conferences and various cultural events. The beautiful garden (16,500 sq. m.) matching the beauty of the edifice, is one of Nagasaki's well-Known spots.

*Madam Butterfly, Chinese Temple,
The Monument of the 26 Saints.*

The Statue of Peace, Eye Bridge.

Nagasaki Cultural Dragon

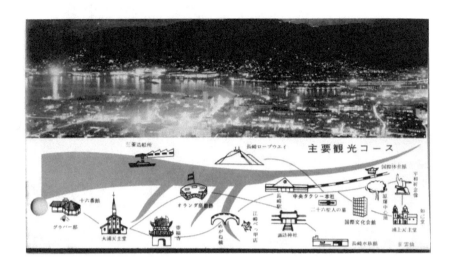

Our Taxi route. Peace Statue upper right.

Nagasaki at Night

Hiroshima

Hiroshima Peace Memorial

Jan 4, 1964 elevator

By Doug Bohs, AQF2/VF-21, 63-64 & 65 cruises

As a still wet-behind-the-ears, almost 21-year-old member of Fighter Squadron 21, I was looking forward to my first at-sea period. In early November of 1963 we flew from Miramar to Alameda in an old R4D. It was the fourth time I had flown but the first time I flew facing backwards. Soon after boarding the largest ship I had ever seen we found our berthing compartments, loaded our Fire Control test equipment into our shop space and found the mess decks; a lot of culture shock in a short time.

Before leaving for Hawaii we sailed out on our Dependents' Day Cruise. The Army Band started playing on the Hangar Deck about the time we passed under the Golden Gate Bridge. Shortly after we reached the Continental Shelf (Cabbage Patch) a few of the band members had left their instruments and hats where they had been playing and found their way to the sponson deck. A short time later it looked as if the entire band had disappeared and made their way to a suitable spot to lose their lunch. In all fairness there were a few sailors with the same problem. We left Alameda on November 8, bound for Pearl Harbor. While underway the "Old Salts" advised the newbies among us on what to expect while on board our new home. This was not done in a sit-down lecture series but was woven into our daily activities. There were several safety issues we were advised of but were quickly learned on our own.

The hangar deck was always an obstacle course of tie- down chains, wings, propellers and horizontal stabilizers. If you made the journey at night it was even more of a challenge considering the dim, red-only lighting known as "brown ship." If you were carrying equipment that prevented you from seeing your feet and what was directly in front of you, another dimension of difficulty was added. The same was true of the flight deck, day or night. Flight Ops also added the threats of jet blasts, air intakes, whirl- ing propellers and prop wash. Landing aircraft rarely snapped the arresting gear but if they did the lashing cable could remove legs. If you were lucky enough to be working aft of the island you were also able to enjoy the choking sensation of stack gas. I must admit, apart from the smell of baking bread, the smell of high-octane avgas exhausted from VA-25's Spads was one smell the Midway offered I actually liked. If you safely navigated your way across the hangar deck your next obstacle would either be a ladder or a hatch. Ladders were usually only a safety issue if again, you were carrying equipment. Hatches had their own set of issues due to the coamings that surrounded them. Ah yes, the hatch coamings, those steel ridges that would bark your shins if you failed to lift your legs or catch you somewhere from your forehead to the top of your skull if you failed to duck your head as you passed thru them. We arrived at Pearl Harbor on the 13th of November and moored at Ford Island. Later that day we left Ford Island to begin Operational Readiness Inspection (ORI) exercises. On November 16th we docked at Pearl Harbor. We left Pearl on the 18th, to continue Operational Readiness Inspections.

General Quarters was a common drill during an ORI. One particular day we had at least three GQ drills. I had just finished my 1800 to 0600 shift and had settled into my bunk for the second time when we had another GQ call. I was still half-asleep and racing forward to our AQ shop. This was when I was first introduced to the damage a hatch coaming could do to your head. I was doing pretty well picking up my feet and lowering my head until I forgot the second part. The next thing I remember was a ship's doctor was telling a corpsman "you can't numb his scalp." I wished he would have spoken sooner. So be- sides the numerous jabs he had made in a futile effort to spare me further pain he put 12 stitches across the top of my head. I can still feel the scar. We docked again on the 21st of November. As everyone on that cruise remembers, President Kennedy was assassinated on the 22nd. Anyone who was ashore when the news was received was under orders to return to the ship. We pulled anchor that day and stood out to sea. It was reported after we left port that submarine nets were de- ployed at the base, I do not remember how long we stayed out to sea. After it was discovered we were not at war we returned to port. The Midway had three main elevators which moved planes, support equipment and stores between the flight deck and the hangar deck. Number 1 elevator was all the way forward, number 2 was located on the forward end of the angle deck and number 3 was just aft of the island. When an elevator went down from the flight deck there were stanchions about 3 feet high with a steel cable running through them that rose out of the flight deck. There were also red warning lights that surrounded the opening where the elevator used to be. Working on an elevator during underway replenishment (UNREP) was a very risky task. The sea between the Midway and the supply ship could get very turbulent, to the point where the seas would wash over the elevator. Personnel have been swept overboard during UNREP operations. I also know it wasn't smart to try to jump the steel cable that came up around an elevator when it was on the way down. On the '65 cruise I saw a reporter attempt that very thing on number 3 elevator. I went to the edge of the flight deck, looked down and saw the result. He was not standing. On the morning of Saturday, January 4th, 1964, Midway lost number 3 elevator. I was asleep in my bunk when it happened. Around 0200 the following morning I was asked to spot one of our F4's for a maintenance check. Not knowing where it was I left the bright lights of our shop, made my way down the ladders to the hangar deck and started my search, still somewhat night blind. After sidestepping tie downs and avoiding everything else that could hurt you, my search of the hangar deck failed to find our aircraft. I then climbed another set of ladders and found my way to the flight deck. It was a very dark morning, either moonless or very cloudy. Anyone who has worked on the flight deck at night during "brown ship" (no white lights) knows what a dark work environment really is. I started my search all the way forward and slowly worked my way aft, again avoiding all the traps that were set for me.

As I recall there was virtually no activity on the flight deck; no fueling of aircraft, no tractors "respotting" planes, or other activity. I felt as though I was the only person up there although I probably wasn't.

The only light you were permitted to use at night on the flight deck was a flashlight with a red lens. Those flash-lights were not very bright to begin with. Couple that with a red lens and you had to be right on top of something to see it. My search had still not yielded the aircraft I was looking for and I was just aft of the Island. My thought was "it might be on number 3 elevator."

When the elevator was lost less than 24 hours earlier the mechanism that held the stanchions, cables and lights in the "up" position was evidently disabled. There were no stanchions, cables or red lights visible. I started walking toward the (missing) elevator, not getting a reflection of anything; not unusual in that environment. After a few more steps I stopped dead in my tracks. No one said anything to me, there was no indication I was in danger; I just stopped. I held my flashlight out in front of me and slowly brought it down until I saw the toes of my "flight-decker" boots. There was nothing in front of them;

no flight deck, no elevator, nothing but pitch black. I was standing on the very edge of the opening where the elevator used to be.

After all of these years I do not remember what was surrounding the area where the elevator would have been. Evidently I walked between whatever pieces equipment had been placed around the opening of the flight deck, thinking everything was normal. One more step and I would have been a mysterious disappearance. Elevators could present their share of danger on an aircraft carrier, especially when they weren't there.

The older I get the more I think about that experience. What stopped me? I have no idea except to say it was divine intervention. An aircraft carrier is a very dangerous place to work.

Elevator gone with the waves.   This is another version below.

However, one wintry day off Japan in January 4, 1964, things did not work out so well. The seas were choppy, but the business of replenishing supplies still needed to so on, so the Midway steadied on base course and the stores ship pulled up alongside to starboard. Guidelines and hoisting gear were run out, and men lined up on the lowered elevator as well as inside the hangar deck to manhandle the incoming crates. Before long, however, the sea between the ships got into the action and waves began to lap up underneath the platform.

Soon, a curler hit with enough force to heft the elevator upwards far enough to knock its guides out of alignment with the hull tracks. Worse, the wave was high enough to crest over the platform with enough energy to knock several men off their feet. Fortunately, no one was washed overboard, but the violence of the hit convinced everyone to scramble away into the hangar deck. Soon, an even larger wave struck, lifting the crooked elevator even higher, and then it dropped away, removing the platform completely away from its tracks. With the entire weight of the elevator momentarily supported by the cable tiers, in addition to the force of the structure's movement, the cables snapped, causing the elevator to slice into the sea. The replenishment evolution was secured, and the elevator bays rolled shut. Though no one was lost in the incident, the practical matter of moving aircraft about with elevators available only amidships and well forward on the bow was complicated greatly.

This situation was exacerbated by the arrival of the new carrier Kitty Hawk who challenged the mangled Midway to an air ops competition. The flight deck crew turned-to with a will, and the aircrews of Air Wing Two pressed on with their bombing and gunnery to wrest the victory from the neighboring Air Wing Eleven. On the afternoon of February 8th, Rear Admiral Thomas W. South, commanding Task Force 77, sent a flashing light message congratulating the Midway and her crew for winning the competition. "Kitty Hawk & CAW-11 are convinced that Midway and CAW-2 are resorting to all sorts of rivalry, skull duggery (sic), rule stretching, outright cheating, shifty tactics, etc."

The ship was still in mid-deployment, and no facilities in the region could replace the missing elevator, so the Midway carried on for three more months with the two remaining elevators. Finally, on 11 May 1964, she departed Subic Bay for a return to Alameda, and then across the Bay to Hunters Point shipyard where she was made whole again. The next deployment would be to Vietnam and combat.

1965.

Nice to know info information.

Navsource.org

She returned to Alameda in May 1964 to replace the number three elevator which had been destroyed and lost during extremely heavy seas on January 04, 1964. This incident happened while Midway was taking on supplies, using the lowered elevator as the transfer point. A surging wave hit the elevator, lifting it and cocking it in the runners. The wave partially went over the elevator, nearly washing off the sailors who were moving supplies. A second wave hit the elevator, causing it to drop out the bottom of the runners, lifted it higher, and then dropped it, snapping the cables. The elevator fell behind the ship and eventually sunk.

June 13, 1963

An F-4A Phantom II and an F-8D Crusader respectively, made the first fully automatic carrier landings with production equipment on board Midway off the California coast. The landings, made "hands off" with both flight controls and throttles operated automatically by signals from the ship, highlighted almost 16 years of research and development.

Aircraft from Midway shot down two migs on June 17 and another on June 20

March 12, 1964
Skipper came in one day with a bandage on his nose from a growth removal.
The following day all the officers showed up with a bandage on their nose.

The aircraft carrier USS MIDWAY (CV-41) conducts an underway replenishment with the battleship USS IOWA (BB-61). This happens frequently. And could be a two-way street. Some of the items transferred are personnel (looks scary), fuel, food, mail, ordinance and one more very important item. Movies. I was the movie officer at one point. Movies were distributed by seniority. Ships' captain, higher on board. Then flowed thru the rest of the squadrons. We would watch these in the ready room during off time, had a very nice lens for viewing. At times we would substitute our own dialogue which was very comical. When done, we invited our sailors in the RR to watch, RR was A/C.

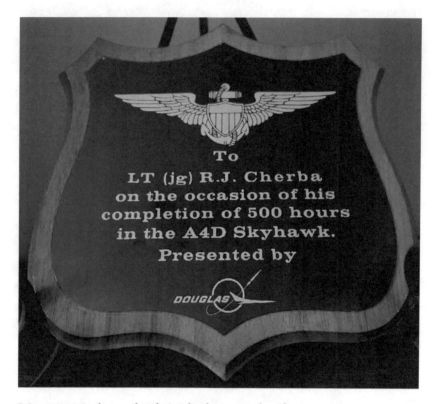

May 1964 is about the date I had accumulated

500 hours or more. I did go through my log book to verify the date.

This plaque given to me by the Douglas Corp. Representative. This is the company that manufactured the airplane. The Rep, who also was on the cruise, was a civilian, who could help the A-4 squadrons with maintenance questions, expedite parts from the factory in the US if an airplane was AOC. (Aircraft Out of Commission).

I think this was Atsugi. We spent a lot of time there.

We were looking at small 50cc motorcycles. We thought it would be a good idea to buy one since it was not very expensive. The only question being was how are we going to get it back to the ship. Well, it just so happened that pilots from the A-3 twin engine bomber squadron from Midway were also out and about. They had a solution. We then proceeded to take them out to NAS Atsugi and their airplane that they had flown in. This a/c had a huge bomb bay that at the present time was empty. So being smart we rope tied the bikes up in the bay. Problem solved. I don't know how many we had but there was more than 1. The only thing we had to do when we got back to the ship was to find a place to store them until we got back to Alameda or Lemoore. But we did and I kept the bike for a long time.

The ship stopped in Sasebo on the way back to the Philippines, Subic Bay. Left Subic for the States to go home. The ship would take the great circle route, Northern Route. The shortest way. Not a straight line across the globe. NWA would take this route for the commercial flights. Depending on winds/weather, usually from states over the Aleutian chain curving in an arc South to Japan etc.

Scheduled to leave Subic around May 12, 1964. On the way home, we had a Russian Bear bomber flying over us. Ship always had two fighters strapped in on the catapults, both, for just this kind of thing. No fun duty. They didn't launch.

A fellow aviator took this picture of me on the flight deck. I think I was going back to my room which was underneath the starboard catapult. It was very noisy there when air ops were launching airplanes. Really could not get much sleep.

This picture was taken after I made Lieutenant. November 1, 1964. Note the 2 silver bars on the collar of the shirt.

The uniform here is work khakis. Had to be warm as a lot of the sailors doing maintenance on the a/c were not wearing shirts.

Notice here also that the a/c are chained to the flight deck. 6-8 depending on the sea state. Looks like we were at sea in the picture. Water visible behind the F-4. The hole is the #1 elevator. In bow.

RICHARD CHERBA

November 1, 1964.
Made Lieutenant

Congratulations from Commanding Officer, Commander Don Wyand

WINGS OF LEGACY

*Lieutenant shoulder board, Midway name tag.
Lighter and a go cup.*

RICHARD CHERBA

LSO (Landing Signal Officer) OfficerOfficer

The LSO is one of the most important duties aboard ship, especially during a/c recoveries. Henry (pictured) was my roommate and VA-22's LSO. Each squadrons had their own because they flew different a/c. As you began your approach, lined up with the centerline of the landing area, a/c configured for landing, you were listening to Henry on a handset and he would be talking to you. Advising you if you were fast, too slow, too low, calling for power, or anything that did not look safe. His handset had a wave off button to lite up the flashing red lights on the mirror. The flags would only be used for equipment failure. As you can see the platform is at the beginning of the landing area. You can also see the cables strung across the flight deck behind him on the left.

There is also a safety net on the left side of the picture (not visible) for the guys to jump into if there was a crash about to happen or something similar. After the recovery was complete, Henry would meet us in the ready room and debrief us on our landing. OK 3, meant that it was a good approach and you caught the #3 arresting gear. And if it was a night landing, the quack, Officially our Squadron Doctor, might be around to give you a miniature shot of brandy. Cool!

The landing aid (below)is the pilots' aid for landing. A source light at the stern (back) of the ship would reflect in the concave mirror and you could pick it up if you were at the right altitude, say 1000 ft. We called this the 'ball'. Also meatball, as it was a meatball color. The on final from you was " Call sign, "beefeater 21, meatball (I see it), and your fuel state. That way the air boss could foretell if there might be a problem if you had to go around and try again. The pilot mantra (scan) was " ball, line up, airspeed. The ship wanted you to land on the centerline. At a point on final you had additional things to take care of, gear down, hook down. Shoulder harness locked. Repeating the mantra. If you should happen to make a "hook up pass", you made a $5 contribution to the party fund. After landing there was a rollback. Hook up, signal from the directors and follow the yellow shirt signals to your parking.

RICHARD CHERBA

This is Henry Papa. VA 22 and Dave Abrahamsen, VA 25 LSO. Dave was in a Spad AD (prop) Squadron. Both holding phones. Barely see escape net. More LSOs. Henry on right standing.

LCDR Stu Corey, LCDR Vern Jumper, LT Bill Clark, LT Hank Papa, Gutierrez, AN, and Gayman, AN, stand by for the first of many recoveries.

Another pilot/LSO landing aid that was added to the A4 was an A/C attitude indicator. It was mounted on the forward area of the windscreen and on the nose gear. This one is a new modern version but the lights tell the same story. The LSO could tell the a/c attitude by visual cues. example would be lining up a part of the a/c with another part. In formation we as pilots to fly wing on another a/c would use the navigation lite on the wingtip with the beacon on top of the fuselage behind the pilot. This would be included in the pilot's landing scan. The red inverted V would indicate would indicate, too slow. Purple, on speed. Yellow, too fast.These lights could also be read by the LSO on the nose gear. Our indicators were red, amber, green dots.?. A simple instrument but not able to remember all.

5) Angle of Attack (AoA) Indexer. The AOA indexer is comprised of three lights. The light indications are a green chevron (v) showing 'too high AOA' at the top, a yellow doughnut (O) showing proper AOA in the centre, and a red chevron (^) showing 'too low AOA' at the bottom. 6) Warning Lamp – Wheels Up. If the aircraft is slowing to land and the flaps are deployed without the undercarriage being already extended, this lamp will flash red to prompt the pilot to lower the gear. 7) Warning Lamp – Terrain. If the radar unit is in Terrain Clearance (TC) mode and the sub-mode switch is set to 'PLAN', this lamp will illuminate if the aircraft is less than 1,000 ft away from the terrain. 8) Warning Lamp – Fire. Illuminates when an engine fire is detected. The A-4 has no extinguishing system so this would normally be an indication to leave the aircraft, especially if accompanied by other faults such as loss of power. NOTE – the two central lamps are used for the LABS bombing system and are not supported by FSX. A GREEN chevron indicates that the nose must be lowered and the throttle manipulated to suit. An AMBER doughnut indicates that AOA is optimum for the approach. A RED chevron indicates that the nose must be raised and the throttle manipulated to suit. At intermediate stages the AOA indexer may also display two symbols at a time. For example, a doughnut and a green chevron would indicate that the aircraft is nearing optimum AOA, providing the nose is lowered further. A doughnut and a red chevron would indicate the opposite.

This instrument is an updated AOA, but I do not know if it was used on an A4 or a civilian a/c.

In 1964 USS Midway & USS Kitty Hawk had a little competition while deployed to 'West-Pac.' Midway was operating with two elevators due to the loss at sea of her #3 elevator. We had the center line elevator forward & the elevator at the angle. Midway won the competition against the much newer Kitty Hawk as attested by the attached message. It's an interesting piece of Midway history......we called it 'Midway Magic.' "Another thrilling chapter in Task Force 77 side by side ops and competition is in the record book. Complete results not yet received however on strength of bombing scores, and at a risk of completely wrecking harmonious relationship between me and my staff and Jack Gambrilli aerial circus, the floral horseshoe must go to Charlie Demmlers aces. Well done. Request Captain Wright procure and present horseshoe at appropriate ceremony. First opportunity send bill to me, I have an idea who will pay for it. Kitty Hawk & CAW-11 are convinced that Midway and CAW-2 are resorting to all sorts of rivalry, skull duggery, rule stretching outright cheating, shifty tactics, etc. but are otherwise acting like good sports. Final competition results later. In all seriousness hats off to two great ships and their great Air Wings. It is a unique honor and a tremendous privilege to be associated with you"

"RADM South"

A letter that Skipper forwarded to us notifies our squadron of well deserved " E " award. The entire squadron worked on this and the Pilots had the best record for our practice bombing flights. This allows us and ship to paint E on the A/C and ship.

RICHARD CHERBA

ATTACK SQUADRON TWENTY-TWO
CARE OF FLEET POST OFFICE
SAN FRANCISCO, CALIFORNIA
(96601)

FF12/VA22/RES:jed
1650
14 May 1964

From: Commanding Officer, Attack Squadron TWENTY-TWO
To: LTJG Richard J. CHERBA, USNR, 644275/1315

Subj: Selection of Attack Squadron TWENTY-TWO as Commander Naval Air Force Pacific Battle Efficiency Award Winner; commendation for

Ref: (a) ALNAVAIRPAC #42 dtg 210202Z of Apr 1964
      (b) COMFAIRALAMEDA msg 220011Z of Apr 1964
      (c) COMSEVENTHFLT msg 241300Z of Apr 1964
      (d) CINCPACFLT msg 282119Z of Apr 1964

1. Reference (a), announces the award of Commander Naval Air Forces Pacific Battle Efficiency Award for light jet attack to Attack Squadron TWENTY-TWO for the 1962 - 1964 competitive cycle. References (b) through (d) extend the commendation of Commander Fleet Air Alameda, Commander Seventh Fleet and Commander-in-Chief, Pacific Fleet respectively for this accomplishment. As the Aircraft Division Officer during the period December 1962 to March 1964 you contributed greatly to the high standards of unit training and performance necessary in winning the award.

2. The texts of references (a) through (d) are quoted below:

   a. Reference (a) COMNAVAIRPAC msg 210202Z of April 1964.

"UNCLAS
NAVAIRPAC BATTLE EFFICIENCY AWARD WINNERS 1962 - 1964 COMPETITIVE CYCLE.
A. OPNAVINST 3590.4A
1. IAW REF A THE FOLLOWING NAVAIRPAC SQUADRONS ARE AWARDED BATTLE EFFICIENCY PENNANTS FOR 1962 - 1964 COMPETITIVE CYCLES:
   VF(F-4) - FITRON 143   VA(P) - ATKRON 115   VP'S - PATRON 40
   VF(F-8) - FITRON 191   VAH   - HATRON 2   VS   - AIRANTISUBCOMIGEE
   VA(J)   - ATKRON 22   GP(L) - LATRON 4   HS   - HELANTISUBRON 2
2. COMPETITION AMONG SQUADRONS IN RUNNING WAS EXTREMELY KEEN. ALL UNITS CAN BE JUSTIFIABLY PROUD OF THEIR ACHIEVEMENTS. TO ALL AWARD WINNERS CONGRATULATIONS AND WELL DONE: VADM P.D. STROOP."

   b. Reference (b) COMFAIRALAMEDA msg 220011Z of April 1964.

"UNCLAS
NAVAIRPAC BATTLE EFFICIENCY AWARD WINNER
A. COMNAVAIRPAC 210202Z (NOTAL)
1. ACKNOWLEDGEMENT THAT YOU STAND NUMBER ONE AFTER SIXTEEN MONTHS OF COMPETITION WITH ALL OTHER VA SQUADRONS IS A GRATIFYING MOMENT FOR YOU. THE AREAS COVERED BY THE COMPETITION ENCOMPASS MANY VALUES, ALL POINTED TOWARD COMBAT READINESS. MY PERSONAL OBSERVATION OF YOUR

FF12/VA22/RSS:jed
1650

SQUADRONS SHOWED SOUND ORGANIZATION AND DEDICATION TO THE IDEALS FOR WHICH WE STAND IN TODAY'S NAVY. YOUR EXAMPLE OF LEADERSHIP IS HIGHLY COMMENDABLE. COMFAIRALAMEDA ADDS HIS CONGRATULATIONS TO EACH AND EVERY MEMBER OF YOUR TEAM."

c. Reference (c) COMSEVENTHFLT msg 241300Z of April 1964.

"UNCLAS
NAVAIRPAC BATTLE EFFICIENCY AWARD
A. COMNAVAIRPAC 210202Z
1. I WISH TO EXTEND MY HEARTIEST CONGRATULATIONS TO THE OFFICERS AND ENLISTED MEN OF ATKRON 22 ON THEIR ACHIEVEMENTS IN WINNING THE BATTLE EFFICIENCY AWARD FOR THE 1962 - 1964 COMPETITIVE CYCLE. THIS OUTSTANDING ACHIEVEMENT REFLECTS THE SUPERB LEADERSHIP, SUPERVISION AND SUPERIOR TECHNICAL SKILL OF ALL MEMBERS OF YOUR COMMAND. THIS FEAT IS INDICATIVE OF WHAT TEAMWORK AND AIRMANSHIP, PLUS DEVOTION AND SPIRIT AMONG PROFESSIONALS CAN ACCOMPLISH. WELL DONE. VICE ADMIRAL MOORER."

d. Reference (d) CINCPACFLT msg 282119Z of April 1964.

"UNCLAS
I WISH TO EXTEND MY HEARTIEST CONGRATULATIONS ON YOUR WINNING THE COVETED NAVY "E" FOR BATTLE READINESS EFFICIENCY IN THE VA(J) COMPETITIVE GROUP. WINNING THIS AWARD IS THE RESULT OF SUPERIOR LEADERSHIP AND HARD WORK AND UNITED TEAM EFFORT. ALL HANDS MAY TAKE GREAT PRIDE IN THIS ACHIEVEMENT WHICH REFLECTS YOUR HIGHLY PROFICIENT PERFORMANCE THROUGHOUT THE COMPETITIVE CYCLE. WELL DONE. ADM U.S.G. SHARP."

3. I wish to commend you for the excellent manner in which you performed duties as Aircraft Division Officer. In addition, your individual airmanship, teamwork and devotion to duty were instrumental in earning many outstanding squadron as well as individual pilot scores in competitive exercises. These scores contributed greatly to the high over all unit combat readiness standings. Well Done and congratulations.

4. A copy of this letter has been forwarded to the Officers Records Section of the Bureau of Naval Personnel to be made a permanent part of your naval record.

5. A copy of this letter will also be appended to your next regular report of fitness as further recognition of this accomplishment.

R. S. Smith
R. S. SMITH

Copy to:
BUPERS (OFFRECSECT)

2

Commander Fleet Air Alameda Excellence Award

LTJG R. J. CHERBA

Is hereby awarded an "E" in

Medium-Angle Loft Delivery

In recognition of his outstanding Flight Performance as a member of Squadron VA-22 during competitive exercise A-11-E in A-4C aircraft at NAAS Fallon on 19 September 1964

Signature and Seal

USS Midway CVA-41

Kitty Hawk (CVA-63) the world's first guided missile attack carrier joined the U.S. Pacific Fleet late Sept 1962 last year. Over 1000 feet long, its 4 acres of flight deck provide a versatile and mobile platform for jet fighters and bombers. This and other aircraft carriers constitute the only weapons system that can be deployed across the entire spectrum of war.

We actually left Subic on May 11, 1964. Homeward bound.

Another story. This happened on one of our flyoffs. I had the Big bomb loaded on my a/c. I had to sign a form that I received the weapon and was responsible for it. I had to take it to NAS Alameda and turn it over to another person, who would sign a custody form. This was to show a record of who had it and has it now. It was off loaded and I think I flew back to NAS Lemoore. ?

As noted in these pages, our mission was that of close air support and delivery of bombs. We also had 20 mm machine guns. Our mission was that of delivery of atomic weapons in the event of an all out war against Russia. All the pilots had top secret clearances. We did a considerable amount of planning for this. We had our own map room where you get the maps needed to plan and draw your course to the targets. These charts were usually WAC charts. See next couple of pages.

From NAS Lemoore the government had routes set aside for practice. Normally about 1-1 1/2 hours long. Called sandblower. We flew these at 200 FT above ground at speeds of about 250-350 KTS. ?

Just prior to the target, we would increase our speed to 500 KTS. The bomb would be delivered in a lofting maneuver (loop). The release was pre-set. Downside of the loop we would go as fast as we could to (hopefully) get ahead of the shock wave. And return to the ship, if able.

Charts had all hazards that were close to the ground, RR tracks, mts, radio towers, rivers, Also airports, NAV info.

Basically, anything that you could run into. These maps are used mostly for low flying. Also cables that were strung across the West side of Grand Canyon. I knew where this one was and was very careful to avoid it.

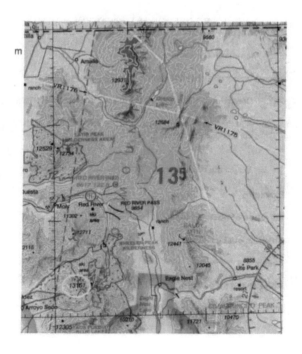

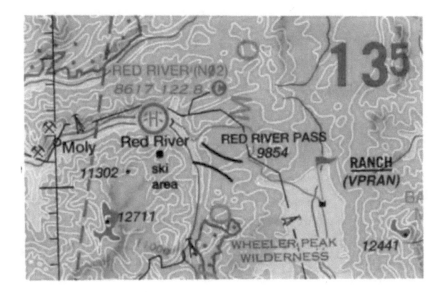

We only needed our map to be about 6 inches wide to fit our kneeboard. And you needed to fix them to discard by a method of your choosing. There were a lot of maps used for these and were all over the place in the map room.

The kneeboard was also used for approach plates or to take notes. The plates below are a Tacan and an ADF approach to MSP. This map shows Minneapolis and Nav aids. You would need more space to go thru the map to explain all of the information that it shows.

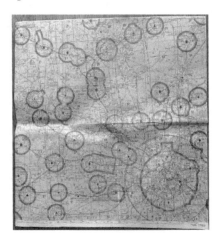

WINGS OF LEGACY

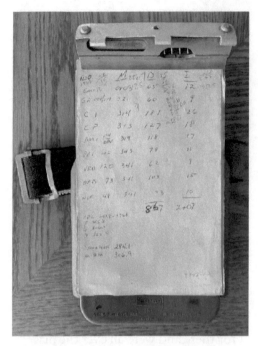

This is my kneeboard. It has my route of flight (VOR navigations stations), magnetic heading, distance, and time between checkpoints. This flight was scheduled for 2 hrs/7 minutes. Information also included ATC contact frequencies.

The charts below are approach plates for Minneapolis. One radar and the other a circling DME approach.

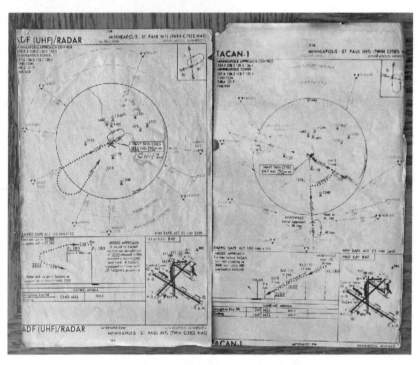

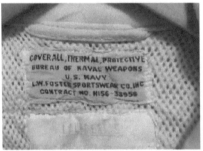

These are 4 flight suits that I brought home. The far left jacket/pants are the liners for the 'poopie suit' that I have mentioned. Keeps you warm/dry in the cold waters of the N Pacific in the winter if you eject. The next one I traded with a British pilot where we had dinner aboard their carrier in HongKong. Note the washing instructions. The white one is the suit we would wear if we were to deliver the 'bomb' and protect us from thermal radiation.

6/27/64

Card from Bass Lake. 6/27/64

Ready room

Relaxing in the ready room.

1st row, Bill Berner, Art Page,

2nd row Phil Butler, Dick Cherba, Henry Papa, and Skip Brunhaver, last Chic Juber.

This was a place we could hang out, have (APM)s, All Pilot Meeting, briefing for our next sortie including intelligence, and after dinner we could watch a movie. Once the officers were done, the enlisted men from our crew was invited to watch the movie also. I was the movie officer. Had to get the movies for the evening. Flag Officer got first choice and then by seniority we would get one. These would come to us at sea while replenishing.

SQUADRON SPOTLIGHT

VA-22

By
LTJG Joe Jamison

Each aviation squadron in the Navy has a nickname selected as a means of identifying itself with the aircraft or the mission assigned. Our nickname, the "Fighting Redcocks," was selected for the original role as a fighter squadron, but is equally appropriate to our present mission of attack. The aggressive little bird, the fighting cock, is the symbol and is symbolism at its best, when backed by the aggressive, can-do spirit possessed by each and every man of this squadron.

Aboard Midway the A4C "Skyhawks" are maintained and operated by Attack Squadron TWENTY TWO headed by CDR Don Wyand. Working with "Redcock One is a total of 16 pilots, 4 ground officers and 129 enlisted personnel. Our squadron is an organization of officers and men, operating with an aircraft which is capable of conducting attacks with either conventional or nuclear type weapons.

The A4C Skyhawk, known as the "scooter" or "Tinkertoy" of the fleet, was produced by the Douglas Aircraft Company. It is powered by a Wright turbojet engine producing 7700 pounds of thrust which has proven very reliable. Although the approximate weight of the Skyhawk is only 11,000 pounds, this high performance, lightweight attack aircraft, carries a variety of external stores, including fuel more than equal to its own weight.

Most of our squadron personnel are in the maintenance department which requires an around-the-

25

clock effort using two shifts. Our administration department handles the majority of the paper work in the squadron and many of our personnel are required to put in extra hours and be on call round the clock.

Our mission as an attack squadron requires many man hours each day, which contributes to our overall mission of seeking out and destroying enemy ground targets. Many types of dives, laydown and loft maneuvers are utilized by the pilot, depending upon the weapon to be delivered and type of target to be destroyed. An unofficial term describing a low altitude bombing maneuver is often referred to as an "idiot loop." This maneuver consists of a level approach to the target 100 feet above the terrain maintaining an airspeed of approximately 500 knots. At a predetermined position over the ground a wings level pull-up is begun. The bomb is then tossed from the aircraft at a preselected angle and the aircraft continues on over the top, rolls upright and continues the dive on the opposite of the approach heading.

A night and all weather attack capability was developed by a technique known as "buddy bombing," which gives the A4C even greater flexibility in fleet operations. This technique is accomplished by utilizing teams of A3 and A4 aircraft. The A3 provides pathfinder service and radar bombing information to the A4 weapons system enabling the Skyhawk to increase the CVA's all-weather potential.

ATKRON 22 was originally formed as Fighter Squadron 63 on 27 July 1948, at NAS Norfolk, Virginia. In March 1956, VF-63 was redesignated Attack Squadron 63 and deployed to the Western Pacific aboard the USS Shangri-la. VA-63 was redesignated VA-22 in July 1959 and delivery of the A4C Skyhawk was made the following year.

Through the years the "Fighting Redcocks" have flown the F8F Bearcat, F4U Corsair, F9F-5 Panther, F9F-6 Cougar and until May of 1960, the FJ-4B Fury.

October 1961 found the "Fighting Redcocks" once again packing their bags, but this time it was a squadron movement from NAS Alameda to our present base at Lemoore, California.

From Norfolk, 1948, to Lemoore, 1964—from the straight deck to the mirrored angled deck—from the Bearcat to the Skyhawk, the "Fighting Redcocks" have changed and progressed. The passing of props, paddles, straight decks, and dog-fights has not erased the need for skill, training and professionalism. Heavier and faster aircraft, fantastically powerful weapons, the tense alert posture of the cold war and our present role in Viet Nam offers a great challenge for the "Fighting Redcocks" as a member of CAW-2/MIDWAY team.

One of VA-22's A-4 Skyhawks stand ready for a launch that will take it on another raid of military targets in North Viet Nam.

26

This article was written bY LTJG Joe Jamison, a fellow aviator in VA-22 and it appeared in the July 1965 issue of Midway West. Printed in the USS Midway Print Shop. Joe's name is on #233 above. It is just below the cockpit and bombs loaded ready to go on another raid of military targets in North Viet Nam. See the Redcock logo and large 'E' on the fuselage.

Ready, Strike, and Heroic Return.

RICHARD CHERBA

Arrived in NAS Lemoore from the 1963-1964 in May 1964. The squadron went through a recycle period of training. This was also a time for some personnel to leave and for new ones join the ship and squadron. Easier than sending them out to the Pacific somewhere to catch up with the ship.

So we did the things like to to Fallon NV for ordnance work. More carrier landings to keep our proficiency up. Had free time also and we had parties, went to a lot of various shows, flew a lot, flew some cross country also. Anyway a lot of training, but time to relax also.

We were required to log at least 4 hours of flight time a month to receive flight pay. Henry and I were always at the Operations Officer desk requesting more flight time. Flight time could have been restricted due to the govt. not giving us enough money to buy fuel.

At one point during my time at Lemoore, I bought a 16' boat with a 75 hp motor. I had a trailer hitch put on my TR-3 so I could haul it around. We could water ski on the Kings River in Hanford. The river had a wide enough spot to turn around in while we could ski.

```
DEPARTMENT OF THE NAVY
BUREAU OF NAVAL PERSONNEL
WASHINGTON 25, D. C.
```

NAVY AIR TRAFFIC COORDINATING OFFICE
TRAVIS AFB, CALIFORNIA 94535

644275/1315
Pers-B126-cmh-2
2 Apr 1965

1. You will proceed immediately and report to Commanding Officer, U.S. Naval Receiving Station, Treasure Island, San Francisco, California, reporting thereat within twelve (12) hours for SEPARATION PROCESSING.

LT Richard KILLIGREW DRUSS, USN, NAVY ATCO, TRAVIS AFB
ATKRON TWENTY-TWO

Ref: (a) Art. C-10201 BuPersMan.
     (b) Art. C-10408 BuPersMan

When directed on or after 12 May and in time to permit completion separation processing prior to 28 May detached DIFOT; proceed first class air completion separation accordance ref. (a), proceed port CONUS, thence proceed immediately and report appropriate activity nearest port debarkation TEMDU connection separation processing. Upon completion and when directed detached; proceed home for release from active duty accordance instructions.

Accounting data 1751453.2254 22/54600. N5E5 250055 CIC 3/5/453/54/50055

Enter in item 11c, DD Form 214: (These orders), 611, Expiration of active duty commitment - voluntarily serving on active duty.

Item 24- TCC B125010; 26; 28(b); 60; 61; 63; 64; 68; 75

Copy to:
COMNAVAIRPAC CODE 61

B. J. SEMMES, JR.

NAVY ATCO, Clark AFB, Phil.
Reported
Departed

Officer-in-Charge

Separation orders. 2 Apr 1965.

FF12/VA22/WAL:eh
1320

13 MAY 1965

FIRST ENDORSEMENT ON BUPERS ORDS 112531 of 2 APR 1965

From: Commanding Officer, Attack Squadron TWENTY-TWO
To: LT Richard J. CHERBA, USNR, 644275/1315

Subj: Change of duty

1. Report to NATCO MATS Terminal Clark Air Force Base, Philippine Island not earlier than 0730H but not later than 1130H for departure on flight CKA P246 on 14 May 1965. Estimated time of arrival at Travis Air Force Base, California is 1510U, 14 May 1965. Upon arrival in CONUS carry out remainder basic orders.

2. Leave balance on 1 July preceding is 60 days. Twenty-one (21) days leave taken to date this fiscal year.

3. Issued MTA Number A-2705190 this date.

4. Delivered and detached this date.

D. M. WYAND

ORIGINAL

SECOND ENDORSEMENT on BUPERS ORDER 112531 of 2 APR 65

ADPO:RCB:js
644275/1315
17 May 1965

From: Commanding Officer, U. S. Naval Air Station, Alameda
To: LT Richard J. CHERBA, USNR

Subj: Release from Active Duty

1. You reported on board this Station at 2025, 14 May 1965 for temporary duty in connection with separation processing. No leave taken while en route this Command or during separation processing. Government quarters and Government mess, as defined in paragraph 1150 of JTR, were available to you but not immediately available to your dependents, if any.

2. Examined and found physically qualified for separation in accordance with Article C-10409, BUPERS Manual.

 17 MAY 1965   D. E. Billings
 (Date)   D. E. BILLINGS, LT, MC, USN
                                        (Medical Officer)

3. As verified by your Officers Leave Record (NAVPERS-329) your earned leave credit computed through the effective date of separation is SIXTY (60) days.

4. Detached at 1300 this date. You are granted EIGHT (08) days travel time computed on the basis of the time required to travel by (xxxxxxxxxx) (private) conveyance in returning to your home of record when ordered to active duty, upon the expiration of which at 2400 on 25 May 1965, you will regard yourself released from all active duty and transferred to inactive duty in the U. S. Naval Reserve. Reimbursement for travel time subsequent to detachment will be in accordance with detailed instructions contained in the Navy Comptroller Manual.

5. According to your service record you were ordered to active duty from Elyria, Ohio and your home of record at the time was Elyria, Ohio. You have elected to receive mileage allowance to home of record.

6. You have stated that upon release from active duty your "mailing address", the place at which you may be reached at any time by orders or other official communications, will be 2223 N. Ridge Road, Elyria, Ohio. Inform the command having custody of your service record as set forth below of any change of "mailing address". Upon your release to inactive duty, your records will be forwarded to the Naval Reserve Manpower Center, Naval Training Center, Bainbridge, Maryland. Any questions regarding your status should be addressed to that command and should include your full name, grade and service number, branch and class of service and mailing address. Should you subsequently affiliate with a Reserve Training Program your records will be maintained by the Commandant of the Naval District in which you reside, or as directed by the Chief of Naval Reserve Training in the case of affiliation with the Naval Air Reserve Program.

7. You are advised that your release from active duty does not terminate your status as a member of the U. S. Naval Reserve. On the day following the effective date of your release from active duty as specified in paragraph 4 of this endorsement, you will assume the status of a member of the Naval Reserve on inactive duty. While on inactive duty you are subject to involuntary recall to active duty to the extent authorized by Federal statute. Inform the command having custody of your service record, in accordance with paragraph 6 above, of any change in health which might prevent active service in time of war. You shall promptly answer all official correspondence addressed to you as such and shall comply with instructions contained therein.

8. In the event that you plan travel or residence in foreign countries for a period in excess of 30 days, notice of intent will be submitted to the command having custody of your service record. Such notice should include destination, expected duration of travel or residency, and forwarding address.

                                        R. C. Brogan
                                        R. C. BROGAN
                                        By direction

Copy to:
CO NRMC, NTC, Bainbridge, Md.
Service Record
BUPERS
Disbursing Officer (2)
Cognizant Bureau (Staff Corps and Aviation Officers)
RORA

Release from Active Duty 17 May 65

NAVCOMPT FORM 2020 (7 PT) (REV. 6-59)
Approved by
Comptroller General, U. S.
March 24, 1958

VOUCHER FOR REIMBURSEMENT FOR TRAVEL

D. O. VOUCHER NO.

BUREAU VOUCHER NO. 123'1

DEPARTMENT, BUREAU OR ESTABLISHMENT: NAVY

PAYEE (Name): Richard J CHERBA — (Rank or rate): LT — (File or Service No.): 664275

MAILING ADDRESS

OFFICIAL DUTY STATION: NAS ALAMEDA

TAD ORDER NO.: BUPERS-11253 T-

PAID BY: MAY 17 1965

	ITEMS REIMBURSABLE	AMOUNT
MEMBER'S TRAVEL	A. MILEAGE 65 miles at 6¢	3.90
	B. MONETARY ALLOWANCE IN LIEU OF TRANSPORTATION ____ miles at ____	
	C. PER DIEM: AS PER ATTACHED NAVCOMPT 2022 5/23-5/26/65	17.28
	D. MISC. EXPENSES:	1.00
DEPENDENTS' TRAVEL	A. ____ person(s) ____ miles at ____	
	B. person(s) miles at	
DISLOCATION ALLOWANCE		
TRAILER ALLOWANCE	A. ____ miles at ____	
	B. miles at	
OTHER (Specify type)		

VOUCHER DEDUCTIONS	Applied to travel advance		TOTAL AMOUNT OF CLAIM	22.18
	Other		TOTAL VOUCHER DEDUCTIONS	
			NET AMOUNT TO TRAVELER	

CERTIFIED CORRECT AND PROPER FOR PAYMENT — DATE — SIGNATURE OF AUTHORIZED CERTIFYING OFFICIAL: T. H. HENRY by P. V. BRANCH SUPVR

ACCOUNTING CLASSIFICATION

Appropriation Symbol and Subhead	Object Class	Expenditure Account	Chargeable Activity	Bureau Control or Subauth's Activity	Bureau Control No.	Sub-auth's No.	Identification No.	Amount
1751453.2254	210	74270		22	54460		[illegible]	3.90 [illegible]
"	"	74271		"			251055	18.28

PAID BY CHECK (Number)	(Date of check)	PAID IN CASH (Amount)	(Date paid)	SIGNATURE OF PAYEE Required for cash payment only
		22.18		Richard J Cherba

Travel Reimbursement

I have included part of an article from the internet, which gives an account of what we did on this cruise. The full cruise lasted from March 6, 1965 until arrival back in Alameda November 23, 1965. NOTE: I left the cruise in May 1965 to go home.

————————

In March 1965, the USS Midway (CV-41) departed her Bay Area homeport of Naval Air Station Alameda for her first combat deployment. Though no strangers to waters off Southeast Asia, the carrier and her air wing were now returning to this troubled region during a shooting war. Operating about 100 miles off the South Vietnamese coast in the Tonkin Gulf at a spot called "Yankee Station " Midway aircraft were tasked to conduct a sustained aerial bombardment of North Vietnam as part of Operation Rolling Thunder.

Intended more to exert political pressure on Hanoi's ambitions than to inflict decisive damage, Rolling Thunder missions were carefully orchestrated from Washington and often neglected the tactical realities of the war and the experiences of the warfighters. While the deterrent objective of the campaign ultimately failed, it certainly kept Midway's aircrews busy during the deployment.

Arriving at Yankee Station in early April, the crew quickly fell into the routine of launching three strikes a day for seven days. Targets were typically enemy aircraft in flight, fuel storage tanks, barracks, bridges, barges, trains, and truck convoys. Although the bombardment had been going on for just over a month when Midway arrived, North Vietnamese defenses, provided mainly from the Soviet Union and China, were rapidly improving and becoming steadily lethal.

Ironically, Midway's first aircraft loss was accidental. On April 20, Lt. Phillip Butler, an A-4 Skyhawk pilot with Attack Squadron 22(VA-22), was forced to eject after the bombs he carried detonated immediately after being released from his aircraft. I was part of this 4 a/c flight in position 2. I didn't see Phil until a 25th VA-22 reunion in Las Vegas. He managed to evade for four days before being captured. As a prisoner of war, Butler helped disseminate the famous "tap code" for fellow prisoners to secretly communicate from cell to cell.

In May 1965, Lt. Paul Ilg, also an A-4 Skyhawk pilot with VA-22, was shot down over northeast Laos during a reconnaissance mission near the Ho Chi Minh Trail. The area's remoteness worked to his advantage, as even the communist troops on the ground could not find him. Ilg spend two days successfully evading enemy forces before he was finally rescued by an Air America helicopter that was operated by the Central Intelligence Agency (CIA) conducting covert operation in Southeast Asia during the war.

This is Paul's successful return to Midway after he was rescued. He is hoisted by his squadron mates. Dan Gildner, Bill Newman, Paul Ilg, Mick Miefert and Skip Brunhaver. A very joyful bunch of sailors.

Dan Gildners' remembrance of Paul's shoot down Follows.

RICHARD CHERBA

It Was a Bad Flying Day

3 June 1965 Thursday

"Yesterday I had the duty. It was a bad flying day. We had 3 aircraft shot down ni the air wing. Two A-4E's and one A-1. Four people died in the A-1 crash. The pilot in one of the A-4E's ejected but his chute did not open.

The other A-4E pilot ejected and has probably been captured.

More bad times today. This afternoon Paul Ilg and I were on an "Operation Barrel Roll" recce. Al was peaceful until we ran into a flak trap. Paul was hit hard. He ejected and the plane crashed within 200 yards of him. He hit in the jungle and may have a chance to get away. I stayed in the area over 1/2hour but never did see him after he went into the trees."

These diary notes were made by Lt. Dan Gildner of VA-22 based aboard the U.S.S. Midway. Paul Ig was Lt. Raymond "Paul" lg also of VA-22. The squadron flew the Douglas A4-C Skyhawk. "Operation Barrel Roll" was a joint U.S. Navy and Air Force operation conducted over the Kingdom of Laos. It was a covert operation intended to cut off or at least slow the supply of war material to the North Vietnamese Army via the Ho Chi Min Trail.

Trucks would be the prime target.

Lieutenant Ig was flying his 29th combat mission on Thursday June ,31965. Thsi was supposed to be a routine armed road reconnaissance mission ("ROAD RECCE"), but that changed drastically.

Lts. Ilg and Gildner were about 300 miles from the US Midway over northern Laos. They were over Route 65 about ten miles east of Sam Neua (Xam Nua). (1) Lt. Ilg was flying at 3,500 ft. while Lt. Gildner was flying a weave pattern about 500 feet above him. Suddenly Lt. Ig felt an extremely hard jolt and the aircraft started a roll to port. With flames streaming from his aircraft he managed to eject before it went inverted. His automatic ejection seat malfunctioned and he saw the ground rising quickly below him. He separated from the seat and deployed his 'chute seconds before he hit into the tops of the trees. This actually worked in his favor as he could see flashes from ground fire during his descent. His chute opened in time for him to make a couple of swings before he hit the trees. Lt. Ilg covered his face, closed his eyes and crossed his legs as he descended into the jungle. All he felt at the time was a soft landing on the jungle floor.

He could hear Lt. Gildner's plane circling the area. Although he knew he had to leave the crash site with his parachute so plainly visible in the trees, he also knew he had to try to make radio contact with L.t Gildner. Staying as low as possible Lt. Ig moved about 500 yards when he heard men approaching.

He crawled into an area filled with thick bushes and fallen trees. They approached from three sides and he heard them calling to each other and shooting into the air. At least two of them closed within 15 feet of his position.

They searched for Lt. Ilg for about two hours in this general area before they moved off. By now it was approaching sunset and he moved out of this position as quietly as possible. As stated earlier Lt. Gildner circled the area where L.t Ilg was downed for about a half an hour. Being low on fuel he had to head back to the Midway. He was not able to make radio contact with Lt. Ilg that day.

Lt. Ilg moved south and crossed a fairly large pile of rocks and headed into a deep ravine filled with a thick growth of trees. By now it was almost completely dark. He came out of the trees at what he judged to be the edge of an enemy bivouac area. Here he spotted several campfires, the nearest perhaps 40 to 50 yards away. There was quite a bit of activity in the area so he waited on the edge of the clearing and slept for a couple of hours. When he woke things had quieted down and it was very dark. In the dark the bivouac area appeared to be somewhat cleared but he could not tell how large it was. Lt Ilg knew he had to leave this area. Rather than risk meeting the enemy whose campfires were still visible on the edge of the area and not wanting to make any noise in trying to move through the jungle at night, he started across the area. Before moving very far Lt. Ilg was "clotheslined" by what he determined was a volleyball net. Before leaving the area he also fell into a slit trench and a foxhole. He was sure the noise would wake someone but no one seemed to hear it. Lt. Ilg was captain of the wrestling team at the Naval Academy. His athletic ability was proving very useful and would be so again. He made his way through the dark for about 3 hours passing close to a road. He soon saw 3 trucks which moved onto the road from a tree covered parking area with their lights on. He could see soldiers in the trucks.

Lt. Ilg was running on pure adrenalin. He pushed on through the night moving as far from the crash site as possible in the thick tangled jungle.

During this first night on the ground Lt. Ilg heard a high altitude aircraft and tried his radio. He was able to make contact with an Ari Force F-101 Voodoo pilot. This information was then relayed to Air America. The services now knew this was a rescue situation.

4 June 1965 Friday

About 5 AM. . Lt Ilg spotted a very high rise covered with thick undergrowth. He climbed to near the top and settled into the undergrowth, pulled of several ticks and leeches and slept again.

Early that morning several planes from Midway were dispatched on a RESCAP mission to Lt. Ilg's downed position.

VA-22 pilots included Lt.Gildner and Ltjg RM. . "Skip" Brunhaver. (2) VA-25 pilots Lt. Clinton "Clint" Johnson, Cmdr. Harold "Harry" Ettinger and Ensign Holt Livesay of VA-25 flying the A1-M Skyraider were part of that group. F-8 Crusaders of VF-111 were also sent to the crash site.

Lt Ilg soon heard propeller-driven planes overhead. Suddenly the entire valley below him erupted with anti- aircraft fire. Until he heard the deafening roar of the guns L.t Ilg had no idea how close he had settled to the enemy's anti-aircraft emplacement. While planes from the Midway were carrying out their RESCAP mission Lt. Ilg spotted T-28's with Royal Lao markings attacking the anti-aircraft positions. Ensign Livesay's personal log provided the following: "Much flak - enemy shot down T-28 escorting helos (aside: later learned these were Air America operatives.) - Saw pilot bail out &plane crash - Pilot picked up." These anti-aircraft positions shot down Lt Ilg and were protecting a truck park.

It was about this time Lt. Gildner heard Lt. Ilg make radio contact with the Air America coordinator. Lt Gildner and Ensign Livesay heard the coordinator advise Lt Ilg to move further south as the flak was still very heavy. As he moved south Lt. Ilg had a feeling his radio transmissions may have been overheard as he spotted enemy troops at the base of the hill. He stopped transmitting which probably confused his rescuers. After what seemed like a couple of hours Lt. Ilg saw two soldiers moving through the brush toward his position. They stayed about ten minutes poking around very close to his position. At one time he estimated they were no more than 10 feet away. After a few more minutes they moved on. Soon after they left he saw three more soldiers at the base of the hill. They must have had an idea where he was hiding. Luckily they did not have dogs as many enemy units did later in the war as more fliers were downed. Two soldiers with just pistols came walking up a path and Lt. Ilg went into hiding again. fI they were looking for Lt. Ilg it was not obvious. Due to the number of enemy soldiers he was encountering, Lt Ig's ability to communicate with anyone to coordinate a rescue was severely limited.

For the first time Lt Ilg was able to analyze his options in terms of planning his rescue with his coordinators as well as avoiding capture. He initially considered a field on the opposite side of the ridge from the flak emplacement as a possible rescue site. He discounted that option as it was still too close to the anti-aircraft position. He then decided to investigate the next ridge to the south. He moved to the near edge of the field and headed toward the ridge. He still had some daylight left as he started toward the tree line atop the ridge.

Night approached as he reached the base of a very steep grassy slope just below the ridge. Here he was able to rest for a short time. It was dark when he started his ascent. The ground was very slick with mud and wet grass from a strong thunderstorm which had moved in later in the afternoon. (This caused the RESCAP planes to leave.) The slick soles of his flight boots were not made for this terrain. He fell several times in his attempt to climb the ridge.

Finally he scaled the worst part of the ridge. Halfway up the slope behind him he spotted what appeared to be flashlights moving about. He immediately scrambled for a bamboo thicket making considerable noise in his efforts. It seemed he couldn't move far or fast enough in his effort to hide once again. Suddenly when the lights were about 200 yards away they al went dark. Was this a sign he had been spotted and they were trying to get closer without themselves being seen? In the daylight he could at least see the enemy. Now he could only guess where they were. For the second time he felt he was in danger of being captured. He lay perfectly still in the thick undergrowth with his knife across his chest for what seemed like an eternity. It was now about 2:00 A.M. and he was chilled to the bone from the rain. Finally he was able to curl up and doze off.

5 June 1965 Saturday

On the third day RESCAP planes were again launched from Midway. At first light L.t Ilg made contact with his rescue coordinator. He continued his ascent of the ridge but now had to navigate through a very thick mass of bamboo, which made travel very difficult. By now he had put considerable distance between himself and the enemy assets he discovered earlier. From this location he could hear aircraft overhead.

After about three hours he broke from the tree line on the top of the ridge. Although he heard what sounded like someone chopping wood off in the distance he also heard the sounds of birds. This was a good sign he was probably alone. He headed down the other side of the ridge as the trees at this location were 90 to 100 feet high and very thick. A rescue from this area would be impossible. Lt. Ilg kept moving while keeping ni contact with the rescue coordinator. At about 4:00 P.M. he found an area with shorter and less dense trees. Once there he felt this was a good place to initiate his rescue. He soon heard what sounded like a helicopter and other aircraft overhead. He made his way up a medium sized fallen tree which was at about a 30 degree angle, turned on his radio and made contact. He fired his first pencil flare but the Air America UH-34 helicopter pilot did not see it. He fired the second flare and again they did not see it. At this point L.t Ilg was able to talk the pilot, Captain Julian Kanach, to an area directly over his location. They lowered a "horse collar" and Lt. lig was hoisted aboard. He had spent a total of 47 hours on the ground.

Lt. Ilg was taken to an Air America "Lima Site" in Laos. From there he was taken to Udorn Ari Base ni Thailand aboard a de Haviland Caribou. The next day a Douglas A-3 Skywarrior from Midway's "Heavy Eight" (VAH-8) flew in to bring him back aboard.

Aboard Midway Lt. Ilg was debriefed by Midway Air Intelligence as well as Carrier Division Seven Intelligence.

He then briefed Air Wing Two on his experience. Lt. Ilg then left Yankee Station and was sent back to the states for a debrief with the Pentagon. After that debrief he made presentations to the Midshipmen at Annapolis as well as the Navy's Survival School. He then returned to the Midway and flew another 70 combat missions while in VA-22.

For his actions in locating the enemy assets which were destroyed, Lt. Ilg was awarded the Bronze Star. (1) Map

(2) Since contact had been made with L.t Ig by the Ari Force the previous evening, the authenticity of the radio contact had to be verified. L.t Brunhaver was authorized to obtain Lt. Ilg's Personal Authentification Code from VA-22's files. This was a code chosen by

each flier which would, by radio contact, verify the fact that the flier was who he claimed to be, and not the enemy leading the RESCAP into a trap. Lt. Brunhaver and his wingman made contact with Lt lIg the morning of the 4ht and verified the code. After confirming the code Ltjg. Brunhaver and his wingman promptly returned to the Midway. This information was then handed of to Midway personnel, probably Air Intelligence.

RICHARD CHERBA

Paul version

In early June, the young naval aviator had volunteered for a routine reconnaissance mission or "road recce" over northeast Laos. He had been on a similar mission previously with no enemy contact.

contact.

"I had flown the same mission ten days prior with no sighting of trucks and anti-aircraft fire," said Paul. "The previous mission probably dulled my anxiety. This day would certainly be different. While flying at 3,500 feet over Route 65, 10 miles east of the town of Xam Nua, Paul felt a tremendous jolt. His aircraft had been hit by anti-aircraft fire (AAA) and immediately started an uncontrollable roll to the left. He was barely able to eject before his plane was inverted. The automatic ripcord release on his parachute failed, and he rocketed towards the ground.

"No time to think. Auto response was to go after my manual ripcord," said Paul. "My chute was stuck in the trees, but my feet reached the ground."

The enemy had seen Paul eject and they immediately began searching for him. After getting on the ground, gathering his gear, and treating a wound on his wrist, he had his first close encounter. Hiding under some bushes, two armed soldiers came within 15 feet of his position.

"They thrashed around the area, yelling back and forth, for about two hours," said Paul. "I thought it was all over three times while on the ground and that was one of them."

Paul began to move slowly and quietly to get as far away from his landing site as possible. By nightfall, he came out of a tangled growth of trees near an enemy encampment. He had a critical decision to make – proceed through the campsite or go around.

"As bizarre as it sounds, my survival escape route was a heading of 190 degrees," recalled Paul. "The bivouac area was right in my path and too large to make it around before daylight the next day, so I waited until things quieted down and went through the middle of the bivouac area." The next morning, aircraft from the Midway began circling overhead as part of a recuse combat air patrol (RESCAP) looking for their downed comrade. If nothing else, the RESCAP drew attention away from Paul's position. "It was a very welcome sound," said Paul. "Little did I know then what the next 34 hours would have in store." After evading for nearly a day, Paul was finally able to assess his situation. He knew he had to consider his options that best set him up for a rescue attempt and avoid being captured.

"Evading enemy soldiers and getting further away from the AAA to enable rescue," said Paul. "I think crossing the bivouac area was fortuitous because the enemy search was focused on the other side of the bivouac area. That was reenforced when I did see some soldiers who didn't appear to be searching." Paul knew, however, that he was far from being rescued and he prepared to spend a second night evading the enemy. In the early morning hours, he once again spotted some soldiers nearby after seeing their flashlights. Laying as still as possible in a bamboo thicket with his knife across his chest, Paul again thought he might be captured. After a few tense hours, he was able to doze off even while being chilled to the bone by rain.

The morning of the third day, Midway aircraft were back in the skies near his position, once again taking enemy anti-aircraft fire. I was able to communicate with the air wing aircraft overhead and soon thereafter talked to Air America," said Paul. "When contact was made he told me I was too close to the AAA for rescue. He told me to move further south to get over a ridge line away from the AAA."

Air America was owned and operated by the U.S. Central Intelligence Agency (CIA) and supported covert operations in Southeast Asia during the Vietnam War. It was also frequently used to launch search and rescue missions for pilots who were shot down. Paul continued communication with the rescue coordinator as he made his way to a position suitable for a helicopter to fly in to pick him up. "There was no planned time for pick up as everything was pretty fluid," said Paul. "When I thought I was far enough away from enemy fire, I let the coordinator know."

Late in the afternoon, Paul came to an area that wasn't as heavily wooded. He climbed a fallen tree to get some altitude and alerted Air America.

"They brought the helo in from the backside but couldn't see me," said Paul. "I fired three flares but still no visual on me. Finally, I directed the helo overhead by its sound. They finally saw me, and I donned the horse collar they dropped for the ride up (to the helicopter)."

When Paul returned to the Midway a few days later, he received a hero's welcome. That early in the war, he may have spent the longest time on the ground after being shot down and was still rescued. Even after 56 years, he still reflects on his month of living dangerously, especially his 47 hours of evading enemy capture in Laos. "I reflect, not with darkness, but with thankfulness that I was not made to endure the

POW situation that so many of my friends had done," said Paul, who was awarded the Bronze Star. "I think often of squadron mates who were excellent aviators and continued very successful careers and more sadly of those that didn't make it back."

Paul served in the Navy for 31 years and retired in 1991 as a vice admiral.

Paul on the shoulders of Dan Gildner, Bill Newman, Mick Miefert, Skip Brunhaver, Tom Murray with the movie camera. This was return to USS Midway after his rescue from Vietnam.

Lt. Paul Ilg is greeted by his squadron commanding officer, Cmdr. Don Wyland, upon his safe return to the USS Midway following his rescue after being shot down. Following his rescue from North Vietnam. LT Paul Ilg is welcomed back by Commander Don Wyand, skipper of the Fighting Redcocks. His arm around Ilg's shoulders, Wyand praised Ilg for his ingenuity in avoiding capture. He said , "I haven't been out here long enough to kiss you on both cheeks, but I'm tempted.

"What follows is a more complete version of Paul's shoot down as told by Paul to a Life magazine correspondent. —

This had been a routine armed reconnaissance mission over North Vietnam. Everything seem to be going well. Then there was a tremendous jolt and my plane, an A4-C Skyhawk, started to wing over to port. Flames were coming out both sides of the fuselage. I managed to get out before the plane flipped over on its back, but I suddenly realized that my automatic ripcord release hadn't worked and I was falling like a rock. I finally got my chute opened just in time to make a couple of swings before I hit the trees. Probably I was lucky a slower descent would have exposed me longer to the ground fire I could see flashing below. Just before I dropped into the wooded area I saw a ball of fire in the distance where my airplane had hit. Expecting to bounce off of a limb, I pulled my feet together, put up my hands to protect my face and closed my eyes. But I just clunked into the ground. After my roommate Phil Butler had been shot down in April, I had written my wife, Barbara, a long letter. I told her if was ever captured she undoubtedly wouldn't receive any letters from me. I told her about the insurance arrangements I'd made to put our 3-year old son, Scott, through school and I explained why I thought what we are doing here in Vietnam is important, but I still never expected to get shot down . Nobody does. I took off my helmet and started collecting my gear. I was bleeding from a cut on my wrist, and it took about 10 10 minutes to fix that up. With the radio from my survival kit, I was trying to make contact with my wingman, who was still circling, when I heard ground troops coming.

I took out my knife and lay still with the knife on my chest for about two hours.The next thing I know it was 2 a.m. I was chilled to the bone from the rain. I reached inside my fatigues and got out my poncho and wrapped it around me. Pretty soon I dozed again. It was getting light when I woke up. Thankfully I was still a free man, and the coast seemed clear. I had a real good vantage point from this could see our planes buzzing over and the flash of enemy guns shooting at them. It wok me three hours to crawl 30 yard and get out of that bamboo, some of it as big around as a man's leg. Everything was rotten and slimy. I could have hidden there for days, but what a place! Finally I broke for that tree line on top of the ridge. Once there, I knew I could be rescued. I could still hear the enemy troops off in the distance, chopping wood and so forth, but I saw a couple of squirrels and heard some birds singing. It meant I was alone. Eventually I headed down the other side of the ridge. At the base there were a couple of small shallow streams. The trees now were 90 to 200 feet high and very thick-impossible for a pickup-so I kept going. Finally about 4 p.m; I cam to an area where the trees were and not so thick. And now I heard our planes again. I scrambled up on 455-foot tree and turned on my radio. This time I made contact. I took a big breath and fired my flares. Within minutes one of our helicopters came came clattering in overhead a hoist dropped down to me. And now, after two days in North Vietnam, I was reeled aboard-as simple as that. I asked for a drink of water, and they didn't have any. But right then I could have waited another 10 days for that drink.

WINGS OF LEGACY

May 11, 1965

By May of 1965, Lt. Paul Ilg was well on his way to becoming a seasoned combat pilot over the skies of Vietnam. Launching from the deck of the USS Midway with Attack Squadron 22 (VA-22), Paul had already flown more than 20 missions over enemy territory during the Navy squadron's first two months on Yankee Station.

But today's mission was an easy one – a multi-aircraft formation flight heading into Naval Air Station Cubi Point for some well-deserved R&R in the Philippines. It was a 12-plane formation with Paul flying the next-to-last aircraft. *Yawn. Get me a beer.*

Tucked into the formation, Paul's world suddenly went from ordinary to extraordinary as the final plane converged "too hot" and slammed into the underside of the young lieutenant's fuselage.

"I was unable to see number 12 approaching because I was focused on flying formation on the other 10 aircraft," said the 82-year-old Paul. "My first thoughts were to maintain control and not hit anyone else in the formation."

Unsure of the damage to his Skyhawk, Paul saw his fuel gauge instantly drop to only 200 pounds, barely enough gas for a few minutes of flying. Luckily, two of the other planes in the formation were configured as tankers and one immediately joined up.

"I was losing fuel at an amazing rate," said Paul. "I didn't realize what the reason for the fuel loss was until Bill Newman, flying one of the two tankers in the formation, joined on me over Midway and told me the vertical stabilizer from number 12 was wedged into my aircraft.

Plugged into Bill's tanker, the duo quickly lined up on approach to the Midway. Paul had only one attempt for a perfect landing. There were many things that could still go wrong: overshoot the ship, run out of fuel, loss of flight controls or even catch fire. Paul, however, remained singularly focused on getting his wounded aircraft back on the flight deck. "I wasn't overly concerned about running out of fuel because if the engine quit, I would eject," said Paul, a native of Lowell, Mass. "Maybe I should have been, but I wasn't concerned about the fire hazard. The flight deck firefighters were ready." Paul separated from Bill's tanker on final approach only two and a half miles behind Midway's pitching deck. He was committed. "I was all elbows getting gear and flaps down, and maintaining the ball as I slowed to approach speed," said Paul. Paul made a textbook pass with his plane's tail hook grabbing the Midway's number two arresting wire. His aircraft burst into flames on touch down, but the engine, out of fuel, quickly flamed out and the fire extinguished on its own. "Great, no swimming today," reflected Paul once he knew he had safely trapped on Midway. "I always had a great appreciation for the A-4. It's like putting on a backpack and it goes wherever you want it to." A Distinguished Flying Cross would be later awarded to

Paul for his superior flying skills and saving the aircraft, but his adventures while on Yankee Station were far from over. In only a few weeks, his metal would be tested beyond what he had ever imagined.

The 1st photo is Paul's arrestment by the cable. The tail hook is visible still connected to the cable. The vertical stabilizer is visible stuck under the fuselage just behind the nose gear. The second photo clearly shows the position of the offending stabilizer.

12 MAY 1965   WEDNESDAY

Yesterday was colorful to say the very least. On the fly off we were going to Rendz 12 A/c in 3 diamonds and make a fly by the ship. The 3 divisions got Rendz and the commenced to get together into one group. The 3rd Division had a mid air collision and one pilot ejected immediately. The other had a bad fuel leak and other damage but got back aboard. The rest of us proceeded to Cubi Point where we had to wait to land because of many A/c with blown tires etc. I can't understand why pilots forget how to land on a long runway after flying off ships for awhile. Well we were lucky and nobody was hurt. Very lucky.

Today I have the Shore Patrol Watch at Grande Island. Should get some sun and eat lots of hot dogs.

This is Dan Gildner's account of the collision the day after. Dan had the Shore Patrol Watch.

RICHARD CHERBA

Lt. Raymond (Paul) Ilg was flying an A4-C Skyhawk bound for Cubi Point, the Philippines. Air Wing 2, USS Midway, was at the end of a Yankee Station line period. The date was Tuesday, May 11, 1965. The complete story follows in his words:

"VA-22 (Fighting Redcocks) had 12 aircraft airborne and joining over the carrier. I was number 11 joined waiting for number 12 before the flight headed for Cubi Point. Number 12 joined "hot" and ran into the underside of my aircraft sticking his vertical fin into my main fuel tank. The pilot in number 12 was forced to eject and was subsequently picked up by a plane guard helo.

"My fuel state was near maximum when I joined the formation but I could see the fuel gauge dropping rapidly and I was streaming a great deal of fuel. Two of the 12 A4-Cs were tanker configured. Lt. Bill Newman (1) was flying one of the tankers and we joined as soon as possible. My fuel gauge indicated 200 p [pounds] of fuel as I plugged into the tanker and did not increase as I was accepting fuel.

"At 2.5 miles out from Midway Lt. Newman dropped me off on the ball and I was all elbows getting gear and flaps down and maintaining the ball as I slowed to approach speed.

"The aircraft burst into flames on arrestment due to the streaming fuel, the engine flamed out and the fire stopped. Obviously I was relegated to riding the ship into port."

Now Henry and I were in our preparations to depart the ship upon arrival in Subic. The shop crew made us cruise boxes to pack the gear that we wanted to ship to the US and our home cities. We both had flown our last combat missions. When we were allowed to leave, I gave my final salute to the flag and walked off. We were lucky in that there was an a/c going out for some flight time and volunteered to take us to Clark AFB, Philippines, Also lucky in that we caught the next flight to the US and Travis AFB,CA. I was qualified for separation on May 17, 1965 and May 25, 1965 released from all active duty. So from May 18 until I finally returned, there was a lot of activity. The letters home offer a brief freedom of what I did during this time. I waited in CA for the USS Hancock to return from the Pacific so that I could retrieve my bike. One was an interview for a job with TWA and did not get hired. Never heard from PanAm. At some point I packed up everything I owned in the boat, including m/c and two large Warfdale speakers. I was quite a sight with the TR-3 driving US 66 home. You could not see anything but boat if you were behind me. Did stop in Kansas City to visit Fraz who was studying after for his engineer's test for the Lockheed Constellation.

Operation Rolling Thunder
"Mid-Air" VA-22 Fighting Redcocks
By Doug Bohs, AQF2/VF-21, 1963-65

The USS Midway arrived on Yankee Station on or around the last week of March 1965. As part of Operation Rolling Thunder, Midway had just completed approximately 45 days of airops. On May 11th I heard the 1MC announcement to ready the flight deck for an emergency landing. After a few more announcements signaling the successful recovery of an aircraft I went up to the flight deck and took the color photo (Fig. 1) you see below. For almost 55 years the slide was in my possession without the full story behind it and almost forgotten.

Fig. 1 Close-up of stabilizer sticking into the fuel tank of Lt. Ilg's A4-C Skyhawk after it made an emergency landing on Midway. Read story below to learn how it got there. Also see Fig. 2 (below) of his Skyhawk.

Late last year I contacted Dave Batson, a fellow VF-21 squadron mate and F4 pilot. I sent him the picture and asked if he knew any of the story behind it. As luck would have it Dave knew the name of the pilot. A little research found him: retired Admiral Raymond (Paul) Ilg. After a brief phone call, a copy of the same picture was sent to him and we started corresponding to complete the story. This picture was also sent to Mark Aldridge of the Tailhook Association. They had been keeping the black and white photo of the same incident (Fig. 2) on file without any information on the surrounding circumstances.

Lt. Raymond (Paul) Ilg was flying an A4-C Skyhawk bound for Cubi Point, the Philippines. Air Wing 2, USS Midway, was at the end of a Yankee Station line period. The date was Tuesday, May 11, 1965. The complete story follows in his words:

"VA-22 (Fighting Redcocks) had 12 aircraft airborne and joining over the carrier. I was number 11 joined waiting for number 12 before the flight headed for Cubi Point. Number 12 joined "hot" and ran into the underside of my aircraft sticking his vertical fin into my main fuel tank. The pilot in number 12 was forced to eject and was subsequently picked up by a plane guard helo.

"My fuel state was near maximum when I joined the formation but I could see the fuel gauge dropping rapidly and I was streaming a great deal of fuel. Two of the 12 A4-Cs were tanker configured. Lt. Bill Newman [1] was flying one of the tankers and we joined as soon as possible. My fuel gauge indicated 200 p [pounds] of fuel as I plugged into the tanker and did not increase as I was accepting fuel.

"At 2.5 miles out from Midway Lt. Newman dropped me off on the ball and I was all elbows getting gear and flaps down and maintaining the ball as I slowed to approach speed.

"The aircraft burst into flames on arrestment due to the streaming fuel, the engine flamed out and the fire stopped. Obviously I was relegated to riding the ship into port."

Fig. 2 Lt. Ilg's A4 on Midway's flight deck showing the vertical stabilizer of the other A4 embedded in the underside of his plane (look directly below the intake). This photo was probably taken from Pri-Fly.

After getting home I applied for a job at United Airlines at the CLE a/p. No hire there either. Dan Gildner always talked about NWA in MN. I didn't even know where MN was. I wrote anyway and they sent me a ticket to come for an interview. After completing some tests, I was hired and my employment date is August 2, 1965. There was a Naval Reserve A-4 Squadron at MSP a/p. VA-811. We had to do some reserve time and this was flying again. After an initial re-check I was qualified to take the a/c on a cross country if approved. Had to do a drill weekend a month and a 2 week drill yearly. Did 2 weeks in Guantanamo, Cuba one year.

*LT DICK CHERBA
FROM
THE OFFICERS OF ATTACK SQUADRON
TWENTY TWO
DEC 62 - MAY 65*

🇺🇸 WE REMEMBER 🇺🇸

The ship is a dangerous place to work. Sometimes there are accidents that happen at work or just walking someplace. At times there are choices for burial and one is the burial at sea. Midway had ten such burials on the 63-64 cruise. I think your burial site may be noted as GPS co-ordinates. Latitude/Longitude.

If you would like to explore this further, there is further information about it on google.

The ceremony is attended by most everybody on the ship and is a formal military service. Gun salute, etc. We had one pilot from VA-22 that was among them and that was an accident on a cat shot.

DEPARTMENT OF THE NAVY
BUREAU OF NAVAL PERSONNEL
WASHINGTON, D.C. 20370

IN REPLY REFER TO
Pers-G251-MB/js

15 NOV 1965

From: Chief of Naval Personnel
To: Commandant
FOURTH Naval District
Philadelphia, Pennsylvania 19112

Subj: Air Medal in the case of LT Richard J. CHERBA, USNR, 644275/1315; transmittal of

Ref: (a) SECNAVINST P1650.1C, Art. 224

Encl: (1) Temporary citation
(2) (SC) Air Medal
(3) Copy of FF12/VA22:JUC:wn ltr 1650 Ser: 420 of 29 Oct 65

1. The Chief of Naval Personnel takes pleasure in forwarding, with congratulations, an Air Medal awarded by the Commander in Chief U. S. Pacific Fleet to Lieutenant Richard J. Cherba, United States Naval Reserve, for meritorious achievement in aerial flight as a pilot flying fixed wing aircraft in Attack Squadron TWENTY TWO embarked in USS MIDWAY (CVA-41) from 10 to 26 April 1965.

2. The records of this Bureau show that LT CHERBA is on inactive duty and resides at 2223 Ridge Road, Elyria, Ohio. It is requested that the presentation of this award be made in accordance with the provisions of reference (a). Please advise the Chief of Naval Personnel (Attn: Pers-G25) when the presentation has been accomplished. Enclosure (3) is forwarded for your information.

3. A permanent document, signed by the Secretary of the Navy, for this award will be forwarded to LT CHERBA at a later date.

H. L. JENKINS
By direction

Air Medal in the case of LT Richard J. CHERBA, USNR, 644275/1315

Encl: (2)(SC) Air Medal BuPers ltr Pers-G251-MB/js of 15 Nov 1965

The VFA-22 logo above is an updated version of the Fighting Redcocks. Me boarding a F-11, Beeville TX. The F-11 was an A/C that did not have a 2 seat version. So the first time you manned one of these for a training flight, you did not have an instructor talking in your ear.

WINGS OF LEGACY

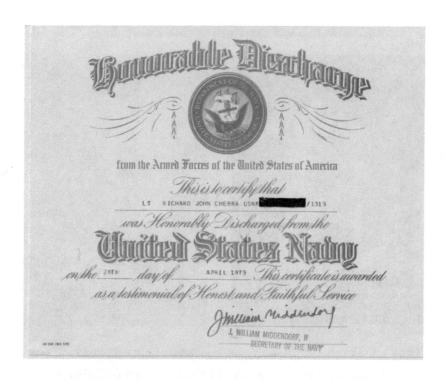

The top photo above is the final disposition of my Navy career. This is after serving in the reserves and so on. April 28, 1975.

The picture of the A-4 Skyhawk with Va-22, Navy and Midway on the aft fuselage. My name is underneath the forward canopy. This was hand painted by a Japanese artist and not a photo. And was painted before I made Lieutenant. The airplane has two external fuel tanks, one on each wing bomb rack.

In the background is Mt Fuji. And then perhaps a destroyer with USS Midway cruising East of Toyko Bay.

Visit to Midway, set up for boxing match. Air Boss located in tower with Red,White,Blue bunting wrapped around it. To observe flight deck.

This is the end of the Navy 1960-1965 section.

There is all sorts of information on the internet if you have some unanswered questions. Google is very helpful that way.

Here are 2 links for the USS Midway Cruise Book. The one site goes directly to VA-22. Lots of very interesting pictures similar to a HS year book:

1963-64, Contents page:

https://www.navysite.de/cruisebooks/cv41-63/index.html

1963-64, Contents page:

https://www.navysite.de/cruisebooks/cv41-63/index.html

Other sources:

library1@midway.org The Midway Museum, San Diego CA is a fun place to visit. Tours, lectures by docents who were aviators, many displays, parts of the ship and so forth.

Midway Veterans Association, Martin FitzGerald

Also a lot of information on the airplane. Google Douglas A4 Skyhawk. Technical stuff, pictures, etc.

People ask about my flying and I have usually answered the best way I can. The one thing I can offer is that the movie, 'Maverick' depicts the type of flying that we did. This was mentioned by an Admiral as being fairly accurate. Go see the movie and encourage your family to at least explore all of the possibilities.

The low level, 200', above the ground was thrilling to say the least. Dive bombing, loop delivery and so forth. I enjoyed the Navy and

RICHARD CHERBA

being part of it and volunteering. Something I always wanted to do.

On this cruise we took advantage of being able to travel around the Far East where most tours do not go. I would do it all again.

Here are some links for the USS Midway Cruise Book.

Here are links for the USS Midway Cruise Book. The one site goes directly to VA-22. Lots of very interesting pictures similar to a HS year book:

1963-64, Contents page:

https://www.navysite.de/cruisebooks/cv41-63/index.html

1963-64, VA-22 page: This goes direct to my page.

https://www.navysite.de/cruisebooks/cv41-63/293.htm

I also asked about 1965. The year I left the Navy. 1965 cruise book. I'm not in this book.

1965, Contents page:

https://www.navysite.de/cruisebooks/cv41-65/index.html

1965, VA-22 page:

https://www.navysite.de/cruisebooks/cv41-65/index_022.htm

CARTOONS

**Hand drawn Copied
from my comic books**

March 6, 1951

Between 1951-1952, age 13-14, I started to draw these cartoon characters out of comics or wherever I could find them I guess. All free hand. There are only 7 that have dates in the lower RH corner. As you can see, I used whatever paper was available.

I thought I would be a cartoonist and even ordered a kit that was on the back cover comic books or ? Part of the kit was a pipe cleaner and that was what you were to use for your model. I decided, after drawing these that this is not what I was going to do. Did some twice.

March 22, 1951

March 22, 1951

RICHARD CHERBA

May 23, 1951

WINGS OF LEGACY

Top January 9, 1952   Bottom does not have a date.

RICHARD CHERBA

April 30, 1952

July 29, 1951

WINGS OF LEGACY

Yosemite Sam

My diary, 9 years old.
1947

January 1-3, 1947

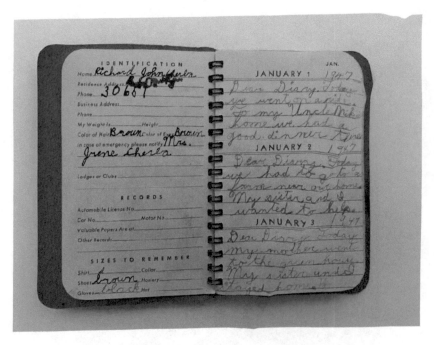

January 4-15

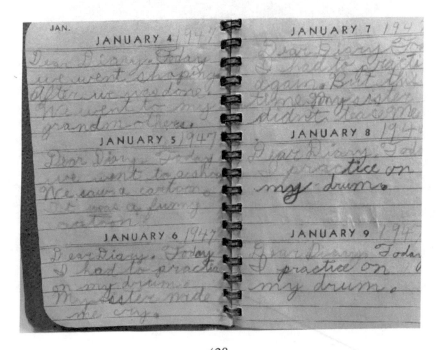

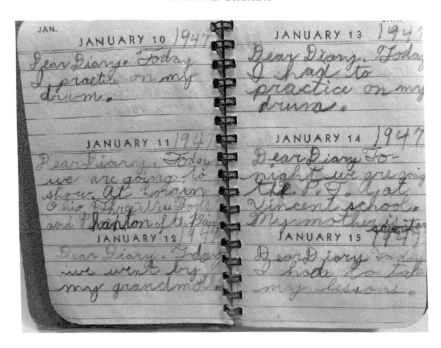

January 16-27

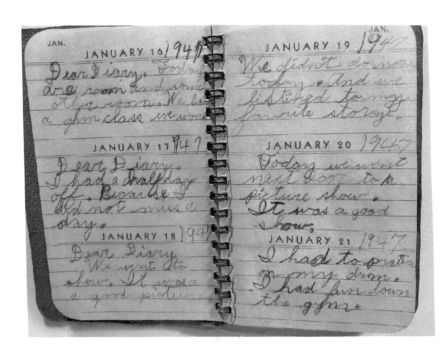

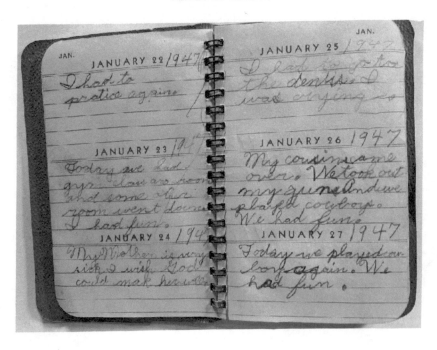

January 28-February 8

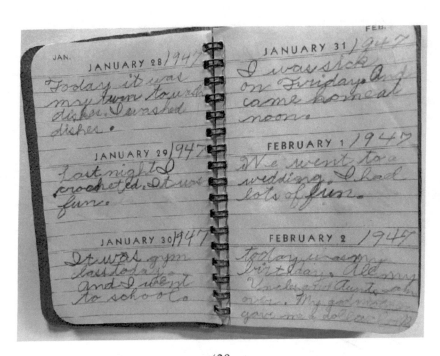

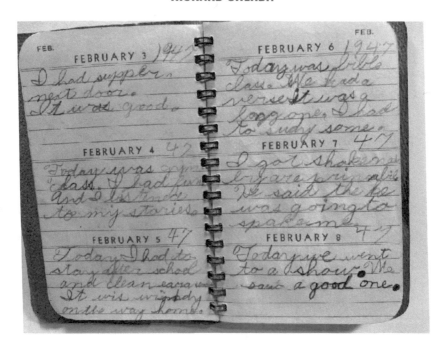

February 9-18

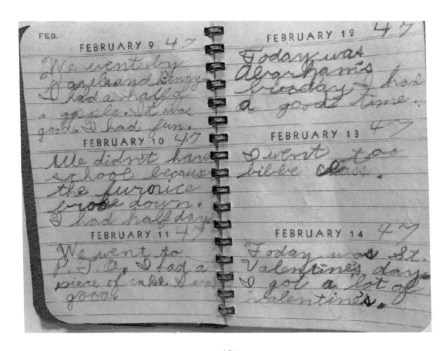

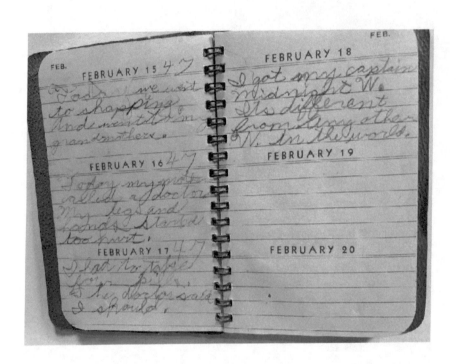

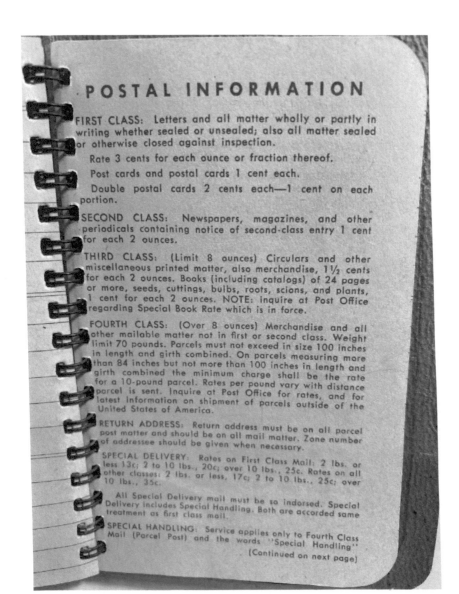

POSTAL INFORMATION

FIRST CLASS: Letters and all matter wholly or partly in writing whether sealed or unsealed; also all matter sealed or otherwise closed against inspection.

Rate 3 cents for each ounce or fraction thereof.

Post cards and postal cards 1 cent each.

Double postal cards 2 cents each—1 cent on each portion.

SECOND CLASS: Newspapers, magazines, and other periodicals containing notice of second-class entry 1 cent for each 2 ounces.

THIRD CLASS: (Limit 8 ounces) Circulars and other miscellaneous printed matter, also merchandise, 1½ cents for each 2 ounces. Books (including catalogs) of 24 pages or more, seeds, cuttings, bulbs, roots, scions, and plants, 1 cent for each 2 ounces. NOTE: inquire at Post Office regarding Special Book Rate which is in force.

FOURTH CLASS: (Over 8 ounces) Merchandise and all other mailable matter not in first or second class. Weight limit 70 pounds. Parcels must not exceed in size 100 inches in length and girth combined. On parcels measuring more than 84 inches but not more than 100 inches in length and girth combined the minimum charge shall be the rate for a 10-pound parcel. Rates per pound vary with distance parcel is sent. Inquire at Post Office for rates, and for latest information on shipment of parcels outside of the United States of America.

RETURN ADDRESS: Return address must be on all parcel post matter and should be on all mail matter. Zone number of addressee should be given when necessary.

SPECIAL DELIVERY: Rates on First Class Mail: 2 lbs. or less 13c; 2 to 10 lbs., 20c; over 10 lbs., 25c. Rates on all other classes: 2 lbs. or less, 17c; 2 to 10 lbs., 25c; over 10 lbs., 35c.

All Special Delivery mail must be so indorsed. Special Delivery includes Special Handling. Both are accorded same treatment as first class mail.

SPECIAL HANDLING: Service applies only to Fourth Class Mail (Parcel Post) and the words "Special Handling"

(Continued on next page)

USS Gerald R. Ford (CVN-78)

VA 22
Cup on left says Lt Dick Cherba, right "Cherbs" (nickname)

I first me Pam in 1966 while on a scheduled flight over Christmas. Pam was a Flight Attendant. I was the co-pilot on a B727, Pam the Senior FA. Since I was single, the Captain had asked me if I would play Santa Clause to his 2 boys after Christmas Eve dinner. He had the outfit and so I did. We took it with us and I greeted all of the kids as they boarded/deplaned the airplane at all of our stops. I even greeted the control towers in Chicago, Cleveland, Pittsburg, D.C. and Detroit.

Over time we started to date. Pam transferred to D.C. and I flew a lot of layovers there. One summer day at my house I proposed to her and without hesitation she said yes. By then I was in VA-811. The Minneapolis reserve A4 squadron. I was able to take an airplane to Pensacola. Pam and her Mother picked me up and I was able to visit them in Ocean Springs MS.

Flew back home the next day. All of this time ,we were in wedding mode. Pam had an MGB sports car, so I arranged to go to DC and pick it up. Also, booze was supposedly cheaper in DC so I bought most of our reception beverages there.

I stopped in Elyria OH on the way to visit Mom and Dad and stayed the night. Left the booze.

I moved into my house on Lake Minnetonka February 1, 1967. Sold it in 2019.

Pam and I lived there for 48 years of marriage and had 2 boys, John and Paul. Pam succumbed to cancer and passed away December 26, 2015.

RICHARD CHERBA

"Something I have to tell you"

This how I was awakened one morning. Pam told me that she had given up a baby girl that was born to her in 1954? while attending college. Jackie, after much searching, finally found her Mother. Well, all hell broke loose. Not really. Our entire family, as well as anyone we knew, embraced Jackie as if she where ours and had been with us since birth. This was a surprise to me and this was the first time I had heard about it. Jackie came out to MN to live. We all loved meeting Jackie.

Stayed with us then bought her own home. Jackie was very active wherever she was. Jackie did work for a while for Pam and I could never tell who picked up the phone when I called the business. In 1974 I took Pam, John and Paul to HongKong. Pam wanted to buy 5 Zodiac cutouts. I asked about the 5th one, but it was because she liked it. Little did I know but she knew. Jackie was only with us for 10 years before she also fell to cancer. 10 years later Pam passed.

RICHARD CHERBA

Ensign Commission
October 21, 1960

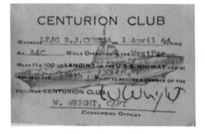

RICHARD CHERBA

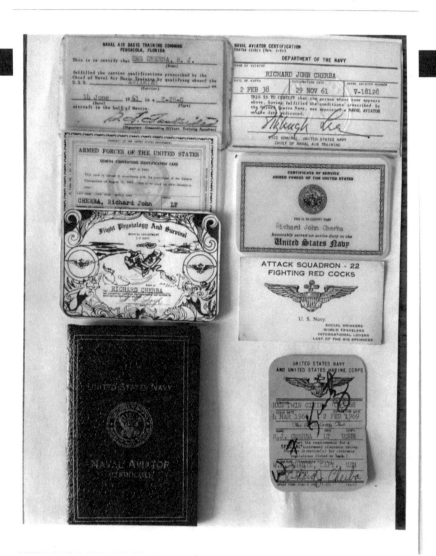

RICHARD JOHN CHERBA

LIEUTENANT, JUNIOR GRADE
UNITED STATES NAVAL RESERVE

Richard Cherba